TENDER

by DAVE HARRIS

Produced by Soho Theatre as part of its 2025/26 landmark new writing season, *Tender*, directed by Matthew Xia, was first performed on 24 April 2026 at Soho Theatre, London.

Supported by

COCKAYNE

CAST

Trae	Kwami Odoom
Geoff	Dex Lee
Donny	Darren Bennett
B.	Jessie Mei Li

CREATIVES

Director	Matthew Xia
Designer	ULTZ
Lighting Designer	Ciarán Cunningham
Sound Designer and Composer	Roly Botha
Choreographer and Intimacy Director	Shelley Maxwell
Casting Director	Heather Basten CDG CSA
Casting Associate	Ella Donaldson
Production Manager	Toby Smith for The Production Family
Associate Designer	Mark Simmonds
Associate Costume Designer	Maybelle Laye
Assistant Director	Wiebke Green
Fight Director	Sam Lyon-Behan
Dialect Coach	Aundrea Fudge
Company Stage Manager	Jodie Jasmin Hicks
Deputy Stage Manager	Emily Davies
Assistant Stage Manager	Andria Digba
Producer	Eve Allin for Soho Theatre
Executive Producer	David Luff for Soho Theatre
Production Assistant	Daljinder Johal for Soho Theatre

CAST

Kwami Odoom | TRAE

Kwami Odoom is a stage and screen actor and award-winning stand-up comedian. His theatre work includes playing Sebastian in *Twelfth Night* at Shakespeare's Globe, and spans productions such as Inua Ellams' *Half God of Rainfall* at the Kiln Theatre and *Barber Shop Chronicles* at the National Theatre. Other theatre credits include: *Queen Margaret, All's Well That Ends Well* and *Hunger*. On screen, he has appeared in *Death In Paradise, The Rook, The Athena*, BBC's *Doctors* and *Holby City*, and short film, *The One Minute Problem*.

Dex Lee I GEOFF

Dex Lee is best known for playing Bear Sylvester in BBC's *Doctors* for five years, earning nominations at the British Soap Awards and Inside Soap Awards. Other TV includes Kenny Simmons in the 2024 Christmas special of *Death In Paradise* (BBC).

Theatre includes: Toulouse-Lautrec in *Moulin Rouge! The Musical* (Piccadilly); Benny in *In The Heights* (King's Cross), having played Jose in the original London cast (Southwark Playhouse); *The Scottsboro Boys* (Garrick, dir. Susan Stroman); and *Father Comes Home From The Wars* (Royal Court). He received a WhatsOnStage Award nomination for Best Supporting Actor in a Musical for *Five Guys Named Moe*. He trained at The Arts Educational School.

Darren Bennett I DONNY

Darren Bennett is a leading stage and screen actor, who has an extensive career in the West End and in theatres across the UK. West End credits: Victor Garber in *Titanique* (original London cast, Criterion); Vince Fontaine in *Grease* (Dominion). Film & TV: *The Royal Variety Performance 2025* (ITV); *Better Man* directed by Michael Gracey (Saban Films); *The Sound of Music Live* directed by Coky Giedroyc (ITV1); *Cinderella* with Camila Cabello directed by Kay Cannon (Columbia Pictures/Amazon Prime).

Jessie Mei Li I B.

Jessie Mei Li recently wrapped production on the feature film *A Rare Breed* and the six-part television project *The Season*, in which she stars as Cola Pierce. She can currently be seen in the Netflix feature film *Havoc*, alongside Tom Hardy, directed by Gareth Evans. Jessie is also widely recognised for her starring role as Alina Starkov in two seasons of *Shadow & Bone*. Other work includes: *The Agency* (Paramount+); *We Might Regret This* (BBC); the Edgar Wright feature *Last Night in Soho* for Working Title Films/Film4, and Ivo van Hove's stage adaptation of *All About Eve* at the Noël Coward Theatre opposite Lily James and Gillian Anderson.

CREATIVES

Dave Harris | Writer

Dave Harris is a poet and playwright from West Philly. Selected plays include: *Tambo & Bones* (Playwrights Horizons, Center Theatre Group, 2022); *Exception to the Rule* (Roundabout Theatre Company, 2022); *Incendiary* (Woolly Mammoth 2023), and *Everybody Black* (Humana Festival, 2019). His first feature film, *Summertime*, premiered at the 2020 Sundance Film Festival. Dave is currently writing the feature adaptation of *The Fortress of Solitude* for Amazon, and an original television project at FX, ABC Studios, and Goddard Textiles. Selected honors include: the Ollie Award, The Lorraine Hansberry Award and Mark Twain Award from The Kennedy Center, The International Commendation for The Bruntwood Prize, and a Cave Canem poetry fellowship amongst others. Website: https://www.staydancingdave.com

Matthew Xia | Director

Matthew Xia is the multi-award-winning Artistic Director of ATC (Actors Touring Company). He was previously Associate Artistic Director at the Royal Exchange Theatre, Manchester, (where he established OPEN EXCHANGE, an artist development scheme for over 400 next generation theatre-makers); Director-in-Residence at The Liverpool Everyman & Playhouse; and Associate Director at Theatre Royal Stratford East. He was Associate Artist at the Nottingham Playhouse alongside James Graham and Amanda Whittington.

Directing includes: *Small Island* (Leeds Playhouse/Nottingham Playhouse/ Birmingham REP/ATC); *The Harder They Come* (Stratford East); *Bodies of Water* (ATC/GDIF); *Skeleton Crew* (Donmar Warehouse); *The Architect* (GDIF/ATC/Stephen Lawrence Day Foundation); *Tambo & Bones* (ATC/ Theatre Royal Stratford East); the Olivier Award-winning *Hey Duggee – The Live Theatre Show* (Kenny Wax Family Entertainment/Cuffe & Taylor); the Fringe First Award-winning *Feeling Afraid as if Something Terrible is Going to Happen* (Francesca Moody Productions/Bush Theatre); *Rice* (ATC/Orange Tree); *The Wiz* (Ameena Hamid Productions/Hope Mill/BBC Big Night of Musicals); *Family Tree* (GDIF/ATC/Belgrade/Brixton House); *846Live* (Stratford East/GDIF); *Amsterdam* (ATC/Orange Tree/Plymouth Theatre Royal); *Blood Knot* (Orange Tree); *Eden* (Hampstead Theatre); *One Night In Miami…* (Nottingham Playhouse/Bristol Old Vic/HOME); *Into The Woods, Frankenstein* (Royal Exchange); *Wish List* (Royal Exchange/Royal Court); *Shebeen* (Nottingham Playhouse/Stratford East); *Sleeping Beauty, The Blacks* (Stratford East); *Dublin Carol* (Sherman Theatre); *Blue/Orange, The Sound of Yellow* (Young Vic); *Sizwe Banzi is Dead* (Young Vic/Eclipse); *I was looking at the ceiling and then I saw the sky* (Co-Director, Stratford East/Barbican); *Suckerpunch Boom Suite* (Barbican/NitroBEAT).

ULTZ | Designer

ULTZ is an Olivier Award-winning, UK Theatre Award-winning, Off-West End Award-winning, Tony Award-nominated designer based in London. He works internationally designing and directing for opera and theatre.

Previously at Soho Theatre: *Touch, Iya-Ile* (*The Second Wife*), *The Estate.*

Recent UK theatre includes: designing stage and costumes for *A Good House, Torn* (Royal Court); *Jerusalem* (Royal Court/Broadway/West End); *Play On!* (Lyric Hammersmith/UK tour); *Juniper Blood, Skeleton Crew* (Donmar Warehouse); *Tambo & Bones* (co-designed for ATC/Stratford East/UK tour); *Death of England Trilogy* (co-designed, National Theatre/Soho Place); *The Corn is Green, Ma Rainey's Black Bottom* (National Theatre); *Richard II, Against* (Almeida).

Recent opera work includes: designing stage and costumes for *La Clemenza di Tito* (Royal Opera House); *Parsifal* (Paris Opera); *Ariodante* (Aix-en-Provence Festival/Dutch National Opera/Canadian Opera Company/Lyric Opera of Chicago); directing and designing *Così fan tutte, Don Giovanni, Anna Bolena, I Capuletti e I Montecchi* (Landestheater-Niederbayern, Germany).

Ciarán Cunningham | Lighting Designer

Lighting design credits include: *Small Island* (Leeds Playhouse/Birmingham REP/Nottingham Playhouse); *Mama Goose* (Theatre Royal Stratford East); *Shake It Up Baby* (Epstein); *The Harder They Come* (Theatre Royal Stratford East); *Tambo & Bones* (Theatre Royal Stratford East/ATC/UK tour); *Sleeping Beauty* (Theatre Royal Stratford East); *Shebeen* (Nottingham Playhouse/Theatre Royal Stratford East); *A Tale of Us* (UK tour); *Stalled* (King's Head); *Tarantula, Gigi & Dar* (Arcola); *Skeleton Crew* (Donmar Warehouse); *Silence* (Donmar Warehouse/Tara); *Cinderella* (Lyric Hammersmith); *Mansfield Park* (Watermill/tour); *Hey Duggee* – Olivier Award Winner (South Bank Centre/UK & Ireland tour); *An Unfinished Man* (The Yard); *The SH*T* (Leeds Playhouse/Bush); *Freedom Project* (Leeds Playhouse); *Me for the World* (Young Vic); *Amsterdam* (ATC/Orange Tree/UK tour); *Blood Knot* (Orange Tree Theatre); *One Night in Miami* (Nottingham Playhouse/Bristol Old Vic/Home Manchester); *Suckerpunch Boom Suite* (Barbican/Nitrobeat); *Eden* (Hampstead); *Last Days of Judas Iscariot* (Vanbrugh); *Dublin Carol* (Sherman); *Into the Woods, Brink* (Royal Exchange); *Wish List* (Royal Exchange/Royal Court); *Sizwe Banzi Is Dead* (Young Vic/UK tour); *Sound of Yellow* (Young Vic); *Sense of Sound: Migration Music* (Liverpool Everyman); *Scrappers* (Liverpool Playhouse); *In His Hands, Re:Definition* (Hackney Empire); *Blackout* (The Dukes); *The Mountaintop* (Welsh National tour); *When Chaplin Met Gandhi* (Kingsley Hall); *Normal* (Rift); *Chris Dugale: 2 Face Deception* (Leicester Square); *Letter to Larry* (Jermyn Street).

Roly Botha | Sound Designer and Composer

Roly (they/she) is a theatremaker, composer/sound designer, performer, and an Associate Artist of The PappyShow.

Theatre includes: *Tender, Eat The Rich* (Soho/tour); *Playfight* (Soho/Bristol Old Vic/Roundabout); *Dear Young Monster* (Soho/Bristol Old Vic); *Uncanny: Fear of the Dark* (West End/tour); *Letters from Max* (Hampstead); *Tambo & Bones* (Stratford East/tour); *The Jungle Book* (Theatre By The Lake); *Shut Up I'm Dreaming* (National Theatre); *Gunter* (Royal Court); *Truth & Tails* (Chichester Festival Theatre); *The Ultimate Pickle, A Sudden Violent Burst of Rain* (Paines Plough); *Half Empty Glasses* (Paines Plough/Gate); *Orlando* (Jermyn Street); *Coming To England* (Birmingham Rep); *Boys* (Barbican/Southbank Centre/tour); *Wild* (Unicorn); *Milk & Gall* (Theatre503); *How To Fight Loneliness, Hir, Warheads* (Park); and *Brother* (Southwark Playhouse).

As music producer/orchestrator includes: *Diary of a Gay Disaster* (Underbelly/Arcola, WhatsOnStage award for Best Studio Production).

As associate sound designer includes: *4:48 Psychosis* (Royal Court/RSC); *Echo* (Royal Court/world tour); *Cinderella* (Stratford East).

Shelley Maxwell | Choreographer and Intimacy Director

Choreographer: *The Boy Who Harnessed The Wind* (RSC); *Coven* (Kiln); *Dream Ballets* (Regent's Park Open Air Theatre); *The Harder They Come* (Stratford East); *Starter For Ten* (Bristol Old Vic); *The Time Traveller's Wife: The Musical* (Apollo); *The Secret Life of Bees* (Almeida); *The Ballet Boyz 'England on Fire'* (Sadler's Wells); *Get Up, Stand Up! The Bob Marley Musical* (Lyric); *Equus* (Stratford East/Trafalgar Studios); *Master Harold… And The Boys* (National Theatre); *Cinderella* (Lyric Hammersmith).

Movement Director: *The Authenticator, Alterations, After Life, Hansard, Antony and Cleopatra, Twelfth Night* (National Theatre); *Intimate Apparel* (Donmar Warehouse); *Not Your Superwoman* (Bush); *The Comedy About Spies* (Noël Coward); *Nine Night* (National Theatre/Trafalgar Studios); *Love's Labour's Lost, Tartuffe* (RSC); *Macbeth* (Donmar Warehouse/Harold Pinter); *Barcelona* (Duke of York's); *Mlima's Tale* (Kiln); *Beneatha's Place, Untitled F*ck M*ss S**Gon Play* (Royal Exchange/Young Vic); *Winter, Why It's Kicking Off Everywhere, Cuttin' It* (Young Vic); *Best of Enemies* (Young Vic/Noël Coward); *Shifters* (Bush/Duke of York's); *Alma Mater* (Almeida); *August in England* (Bush); *J'Ouvert* (Harold Pinter); *Macbeth* (Shakespeare's Globe); *King Hedley II* (Stratford East); *Cougar, Dealing With Clair* (Orange Tree); *Faustus* (Headlong at Lyric & Birmingham Repertory Theatre); *A Streetcar Named Desire* (Nuffield, Southampton); *Apologia* (English Theatre Frankfurt); *Grey* (Ovalhouse); *Rules for Living* (Royal & Derngate/The Rose, Kingston).

TV & film includes: *28 Years Later: The Bone Temple* (Sony); *The Witcher* (Netflix); *Anansi Boys* (Amazon); *Joan* (ITV); *The Marvels* (Disney); *Romeo and Juliet* (Sky Arts/PBS/NT); *ear for eye* (BBC/Fruit Tree Media).

Shelley Maxwell won the award for Best Choreographer at the inaugural Black British Theatre Awards in 2019 for her work on *Equus*.

Heather Basten CDG CSA | Casting Director

Heather Basten is an award-winning casting director working across film, television, theatre, and commercials. She is best known for casting the A24/Showtime series *Dreaming Whilst Black*, an International Emmy®–nominated production, and was nominated for Best Casting by the Royal Television Society in 2023, followed by BIFA and BBTA nominations in 2024.

Her screen work includes collaborations with leading studios and filmmakers such as James Watkins, Jada Pinkett Smith, Rob Savage, Luca Guadagnino, and Liesl Tommy. Recent credits include *Speak No Evil* for Universal/ Blumhouse, the Venice-winning BBC feature *Hoard*, and the Universal feature *Other Mommy.*

In theatre, Basten has cast productions across the West End and major regional stages, including *One Flew Over's The Cuckoo's Nest* (The Old Vic), Harold Pinter's *The Homecoming* directed by Matthew Dunster (Young Vic); *Elektra* starring Brie Larson and *Barcelona* directed by Lynette Linton (Duke of York's Theatre). Musical theatre credits include *Bliss* (ATG); *A Face in the Crowd* (Young Vic); and *The Boy Who Harnessed the Wind* (RSC).

She is a member of the Casting Directors' Guild and the Casting Society of America.

Ella Donaldson | Casting Associate

Ella started her casting journey at Shakespeare's Globe, assisting on 20 productions for The Globe Theatre & Sam Wanamaker Playhouse from 2022–2024.

Recent projects as Casting Associate for Heather Basten Casting include: *An Ideal Husband* (Lyric Theatre Hammersmith); *Bliss: The Musical* (ATG); *The Boy Who Harnessed The Wind* (RSC/Soho Place); *Lifegame* (Improbable/Good Chance); *One Flew Over The Cuckoo's Nest* (Old Vic); *Tender* (Soho).

Further Casting Assistant credits: *1536, Romans, A Novel* (Almeida); *The Hunger Games on Stage* (Troubadour, Canary Wharf); *Entertaining Mr Sloane* (Young Vic); *Hamlet* (Chichester Festival Theatre); *The History Boys* (Theatre Royal Bath/tour); *Reverberation* (Bristol Old Vic). She is also a probationary member of The Casting Director's Guild.

Toby Smith for The Production Family | Production Manager

The Production Family deliver a variety of theatre, dance and live experiences in the UK and across the globe. Recent credits: Manchester International Festival; Museum of Austerity for English Touring Theatre. Upcoming projects include large-scale immersive touring experiences and 'The Other Place' at the Shed, New York and the spring season at Soho Theatre.

Mark Simmonds | Design Associate

Mark Simmonds trained on the Motley Theatre Design Course. His designs for theatre include: *The Planets* and *Into the Ferment* (Birmingham Royal Ballet); *Princess Amazonia* (Grande Halle de la Villette, Paris); *Fall Forest* (Deloitte Ignite at the Royal Opera House); *Assassins, Little Women* (Vanburgh Theatre RADA); *Richard III, Twelfth Night, A Midsummer Night's Dream* (Guildhall School of Music and Drama). As Associate Designer projects include: *Jerusalem* (Royal Court/Apollo); *La Clemenza Di Tito* (Royal Opera House); *Die Zauberflöte* (Staatsoper Unter den Linden Berlin); *Parsifal* (Opera National de Paris); *Ariodante* (le Festival d'Aix en Provence).

Maybelle Laye | Costume Associate

Maybelle Laye studied Costume Construction at RADA and graduated with Distinction in 2019. As well as designing, she also works as a Costume Supervisor and has costumed many shows across London and England.

Credits include: *Richard III* (Costume Designer – Liverpool Playhouse); *Cinderella* (Costume Designer – Brixton House); *The House Party* (Costume Designer – Chichester Festival Theatre); *A Raisin in the Sun* (Costume Designer – Lyric/Leeds Playhouse); *Love Play* (Costume Designer – Guildhall); *A Strange Loop* (Associate Costume Designer – Barbican); *Play On* (Associate Costume Designer – Belgrade); *The Wiz* (Associate Costume Designer – Hope Mill); *The Great* Season 2 & 3 (MRC/HULU); *Bad Sisters* (Apple TV/Merman Productions); *Silo* (MRC/Apple TV); *The Kindness of Strangers* (independent short film); *Eve* (independent short film).

Wiebke Green | Assistant Director

Wiebke trained at the Orange Tree Theatre and as intern director to Katie Mitchell on *Orlando* (Schaubühne) and *Anatomie eines Suizids* (Schauspielhaus Hamburg).

Her recent work includes: *Tarantula, Dear Martin, Union* (Arcola); *The Heresy of Love* (Rose Bruford); *The Journey to Venice* (Finborough); *In the Forest of Starlight and Shrapnel* (RWCMD); *The Poltergeist* (Southwark Playhouse).

Her assistant directing includes: *Scrounger* (dir. Lily McLeisch, Finborough); *Dealing With Clair* (dir. Richard Twyman, Orange Tree); *The Frontier Trilogy* (dir. Jethro Compton, Edinburgh Fringe).

Sam Lyon-Behan | Fight Director

Fight Director theatre credits include: *Les Liasions Dangereuses, The Other Place, Coriolanus, Here We Are* (National Theatre); *American Psycho, Moon for the Misbegotten, 1536, Cat on a Hot Tin Roof* (Almeida); *Natasha, Pierre & The Great Comet of 1812, Fear of 13* (Donmar Warehouse); *Deep Azure, Macbeth* (Shakespeare's Globe); *The Spy Who Came in from the Cold* (@Sohoplace); *Paranormal Activity* (Ambassadors); *Choir Boy* (Stratford East); *Inspector Morse, 101 Dalmatians* (UK tour); *Blithe Spirit* (Salisbury Playhouse); *£1 Thursdays* (Finborough); *Dick Whittington* (Queen's Theatre Hornchurch); *Gunpowder Plot* (Tower of London); *Candida* (Orange Tree); *The Omission of the Family Coleman* (Theatre Royal Bath).

Associate Fight Director theatre credits include: *Stranger Things: First Shadow, Les Misérables, Sister Act, Phantom of the Opera* (West End); *House of Shades, Hamlet* (Almeida); *Till The Stars Come Down* (National Theatre/West End); *Heathers* (The Other Palace Theatre).

Television and film credits include: *Mobland*; *Vikings*; *Black Doves*; *Red Eye*; *Masters of the Air*; *London Kills*; *The Pact*; *Pobol Y Cwm*; *Hidden/Craith*; *Bugonia*; *Bad Day at the Office*; *In The Grey*; *The Ministry of Ungentlemanly Warfare*; *Jackdaw*; *The Marvels*.

Games credits include: *Norse*; *Elder Scrolls Online*.

Aundrea Fudge I Dialect Coach

Aundrea Fudge is an accent/dialect and speech coach from New York. She currently teaches and runs accent workshops for The Royal Central School of Speech and Drama and Guildhall School of Music and Drama.

Theatre includes: *Man and Boy* (National Theatre); *Good Night, Oscar* (Barbican); *The Hunger Games* (Troubadour Canary Wharf); *Hercules* (Theatre Royal Drury Lane); *Driftwood, Fat Ham, The New Real* (RSC); *Shadowlands* (Aldwych); *Choir Boy, Here There are Blueberries, The Harder They Come* (Stratford East); *The Lion King* (Lyceum); *Deep Azure, The Crucible* (Shakespeare's Globe); *Clueless* (Trafalgar); *Slave Play* (Noël Coward); *Evening All Afternoon, Fear of 13, Skeleton Crew, Clyde's* (Donmar Warehouse); *The Beautiful Future Is Coming, Reverberation, Choir Boy* (Bristol Old Vic); *The House Party* (Chichester Festival Theatre); *A Raisin in the Sun, A View from the Bridge* (UK tour/Headlong); *Vincent in Brixton, Poor Clare, In Praise of Love, Here In America, Red Speedo, Meeting, Yellowman* (Orange Tree); *Shucked, The Enormous Crocodile, Once On This Island* (Regent's Park Open Air); *The Assembled Parties, East Is South, Between Riverside and Crazy, Blackout Songs* (Hampstead); *Wish You Were Here, Bootycandy* (Gate); *Start Swimming!* (Young Vic); *Refilwe* (Bernie Grant Arts Centre); *Cinderella* (Brixton House); *Driving Miss Daisy* (Barn Theatre); *Bring It On! The Musical* (Southbank Centre).

Film includes: *Bernard & The Genie; Locked In*; *Wheel of Time.*

TV includes: *The Buccaneers* (Season 2 and 3); *Andor* (Season 2).

Jodie Jasmin Hicks I Company Stage Manager

Jodie Jasmin Hicks is a freelance stage manager from Cambridgeshire. She has worked across a range of productions including national tours, pantomimes and in-house productions.

Theatre includes: *The Virgins* (Soho); *Even More... Ghost Stories by Candelight* (UK tour); *Millennium Girls* (Brixton House); *The Gel* (New Diorama); *Still The Hours* (Hampton Court Palace); *Sleeping Beauty* (New Wolsey); *Luna Loves Library Day: The Musical* (UK tour); *Solomon* (JW3/ Stanley Arts); *In the Sick of It* (Assembly Rooms, Edinburgh); *Girlhood* (Greenside, Edinburgh); *No More Numbers!* (Mercury); *Cinderella* (Saffron Hall); *Flood* (UK tour).

Emily Davies I Deputy Stage Manager

Emily Davies is an experienced freelance stage manager. Having worked across a wide range of productions including musicals, immersive theatre, UK tours and in-house productions. Emily is passionate about fostering a creative and welcoming space for all.

A shout out to my family and my Luke, I appreciate you.

Theatre credits include: *Please Do Not Touch* (UK tour); *A Christmas Carol* (Birmingham REP/Alexandra Palace); *The Harder They Come* (Theatre Royal Stratford East); *Tosca* (Clonter Opera); *Stars* (Brixton House); *Piaf* (Watermill); *Romeo and Juliet* (Guildford Shakespeare Company); *The Lion, the Witch and the Wardrobe, Of Mice and Men, Tartuffe* (Birmingham REP); *Grease: Live Experience* (Secret Cinema.)

Andria Digba I Assistant Stage Manager

Andria is a multidisciplinary creative working across stage management, events, and community projects. Her work is rooted in bringing productions to life behind the scenes while creating spaces where young artists feel seen and supported. She is passionate about connecting theatre and community, and encouraging a deeper appreciation for the many moving parts that shape creative work.

David Luff I Executive Producer for Soho Theatre

David Luff is an independent theatre producer who works across the subsidised and commercial sectors. He was Producer, Head of Theatre and Creative Director at Soho Theatre from 2012 to 2025. Notable world premiere productions he produced for Soho Theatre include the Olivier Award-winning *Boy on the Verge of Tears* by Sam Grabiner directed by James Macdonald; *My English Persian Kitchen* by Hannah Khalil from an original story by Atoosa Sepehr; *Age is a Feeling by* Haley McGee directed by Adam Brace; *Typical* by Ryan Calais Cameron; and new shows from Kim Noble and Lucy McCormick. Alongside DryWrite he produced the revivals and world tours of *Fleabag* by Phoebe Waller-Bridge and its New York and West End transfers. With his producing partner Patrick Myles he commissioned and produced the world premiere of *Network* by Lee Hall, directed by Ivo van Hove at the National Theatre before transferring to the Belsaco Theatre on Broadway, winning Olivier and Tony Awards. They subsequently commissioned and produced the world premiere stage adaptation of Stanley Kubrick's *Dr. Strangelove,* adapted by Armando Iannucci and Sean Foley, starring Steve Coogan, playing in the West End and Dublin's Bord Gáis Energy Theatre.

SOHO THEATRE

About Soho Theatre

Soho Theatre is London's most vibrant producer of new theatre, comedy and cabaret. A charity and social enterprise, we're driven by a passion for working with bold stories and distinctive artists, connecting them with audiences in original style and creating memorable nights out.

From our early roots in the radical 1970s Soho Poly, we've grown – and grown – from a tiny fringe space into a widely influential cultural organisation operating across our four London performance spaces; through international touring and collaborations with India and elsewhere; as festival regulars from Edinburgh Festival Fringe to Melbourne International Comedy Festival; and filming shows and creating our own digital work seen across social platforms and inflight.

Alongside working with some of the most exciting theatre-makers and comedians in the world, we also nurture the next generation of artists through a thriving range of artist and talent development programmes, artists under commission and in development, and two new writing awards including UK's longest established playwriting prize, the Verity Bargate Award.

In 2025 we celebrated 25 years at our central London venue Soho Theatre – described by Phoebe Waller-Bridge as the 'the mothership of new artists', Ryan Calais Cameron as 'a major launchpad' and Bryony Kimmings as 'an extraordinary place for people whose work is genre-pushing' – whilst opening London's newest venue, the 'jaw-dropping 1000 seat new theatre' (*Time Out*), Soho Theatre Walthamstow in May 2025.

sohotheatre.com I @sohotheatre I @sohotheatreindia

SOHO THEATRE STAFF

EXECUTIVE & SENIOR TEAM

CEO & Executive Director
Mark Godfrey

Co-Executive Director
Sam Hansford

Co-Creative Directors
Rose Abderabbani (Theatre Programme)
Steve Lock (Comedy)
Jessica Draper (Creative Engagement)

Operations Director
Edel McGrath

Co-Audience & Communications Directors
Peter Flynn, Kelly Fogarty

Fundraising and Partnerships Director
Bhavita Bhatt

Head of Food & Beverage
Scott Viney

TEAMS

Executive Assistant
Annie Jones

Theatre
Eve Allin, Alessandro Babalola, Max Elton, Pooja Sivaraman, Paul Sirett, Maddie Wilson, Daljinder Johal, Ellen Ritchie

Comedy
Kathryn Craigmyle, Lee Griffiths, Jet Vevers, Lola Ferguson, Eilis Woods

Creative Engagement
Jenny Bakst, Jules Haworth, Shazad Khalid, Déviniat Adedibu

Press & PR
Augustin Wecxsteen, Ruby Willis, Lou Doyle

Marketing
Kia Noakes, Sophie Coke-Steel, Flo Granger, Ben Fallaci

Graphic Design
Conor Jatter, Ludmila Bogatchek

Digital
Rhys Matthews, Laura-Inès Wilson, Jody Davies

Audience & Sales
Mariko Primarolo, Jack Cook, Fuad Ahammed, Lainey Alexander, Kitty Smith, Luke Talboys, Sophie Greaves, Sami Sumaria, Erin Handford, Catriona Davidson, Joel Lockhart

Operations
Paul Symes, Laura Schofield, Em Carr, Dee Lindo, Louisa Pennell, Luca Newman

Technical
Stefan Andrews, Rob Johnson, Ben Goodwin, Tom Younger, Lydia Edwards, Charlie Leslie, Aidan Walker, Zac Brewin, Finley Dickins

Food & Beverage
Rishay Naidoo, Ronnie Matczuk, Damian Regan, Evan Jones, Nes Dyer, Abin Marson, Cazz Regan, MD Ridoy Khan, Lisa Gilroy, Georgia Pierce

Audience Team Soho
Mischa Alexander, Erol Arguden, Brenton Arrendell, Farah Ashraf, Aiyana Bartlett, Ellie Bibby, Iona Brown, Auriella Campolina, Becca Carr, Geri Carr, Lanre Danmola, Anais Dos Santos, Bronya Doyle, Gabriel Harris, Oscar Holloway, Andrew Houghton, Hana Jennings, Lee King-Brown, Mariama Mansary, Tilly Marples, Faith Martin, India Martin, Kit Miles, Eve Millward, Benji Morris, Paul Murphy, Fiona Oakley, Jack Parry, Janisha Perera, Jesse Phillippi, Rosie Revan, Alexis Sakellaris, Genevieve Sabherwal, Genevieve Sinha, Johnie Spillane, Dylan Sweet, Abby Timms, Lauren Tranter, Jade Warner-Clayton, Joanne Williams, Arthur Yang

Technical Team Soho
Liz Barker, Bryn Jones, Jordan Lewis, Jem Rohde, Abbie Sage, Han Sayles, Maddie Whiffin

Soho Theatre Bar
Sneha Adhikari, Anand Choudhary, Mike Giraldo Cifuentes, Sofia Dixon, Benjamin Jones, Bibin Gopi, Caleb Seed, Madeleine Hilton, Dizolele Isaac, Tayafur Rahman, Anandhu Sudhakaran, Flynn Tovey Ashforth, Sian Walsh, Chi Whon Won, Zaza Wright, Shambhavi Vashistha

SOHO THEATRE SUPPORTERS

Principal Supporters
Hedley and Fiona Goldberg
Michael and Isobel Holland
Linda Keenan
Soho Circle

Supporting Partners
Matthew Bunting
Stephen Garrett
Angela Hyde-Courtney
Phil & Jane Radcliff
Jonathan Rees

Corporate Sponsors
Adnams Southwold
Bargate Murray
Character Seven
Financial Express
NBC Universal International Studios
Soho Estates

Trusts & Foundations
The 29th May 1961 Charitable Trust
The Andor Charitable Trust
Bloomberg Philanthropies
Bruce Wake Charitable Trust
The Boris Karloff Charitable Foundation
The Boshier-Hinton Foundation
Chapman Charitable Trust
The Charlotte Bonham-Carter Charitable Trust
The D'Oyly Carte Charitable Trust
Dominic Webber Trust – Core Values
The Fenton Arts Trust
Fidelio Charitable Trust
Garrick Charitable Trust
The Goldsmiths' Company
Harold Hyam Wingate Foundation
Hyde Park Place Estate Charity
The Ian Mactaggart Trust
The Idlewild Trust
The John Thaw Foundation
John Lyon's Charity
KKL Charity
The Kobler Trust
Lara Atkin Charitable Foundation
The Leche Trust
The Mackintosh Foundation
Mohamed S. Farsi Foundation
#My Westminster Fund
Noël Coward Foundation
The Peggy Ramsay Foundation
The Rose Foundation
The Royal Victoria Hall Foundation
Santander Foundation
Schroder Charity Trust
The St James's Piccadilly Charity
Tallow Chandlers Benevolent Fund
The Teale Charitable Trust
The Thistle Trust
Unity Theatre Charitable Trust

Soho Theatre Performance Friends
Ali Braithwaite
Anna Bordon
Amanda Rajkumar
Helen Evans
Bhags Sharma
Rich Thorpe
Chris Thomas
Gary Wilder

Soho Theatre Playwright Friends
Maital Dar
Mrs Emily Fletcher
Liam Goddard
Andrew Lucas
Emma Whitting

TENDER

Dave Harris

'I am a grown man
excuse the buttery light haloing my head'

Kaveh Akbar,
from Calling a Wolf a Wolf

Characters

TRAE, *He/Him. Soft one. Young hot. Acrobat.*
GEOFF, *He/Him. Hard bull. Arrogant hot. Athlete.*
DONNY, *He/Him. Oldest. Dad hot. Doesn't dance.*
B., *She/They. Someone who is inaccessibly beautiful.*

Setting

Here.

Note

Upon entering the theater, audience members should be provided a paddle.

One side is green and one side is red.

Anyone who is comfortable being touched should wave their green paddles when the moment calls for it.

This text went to press before the end of rehearsals and so may differ slightly from the play as performed.

The back room of a performance club that used to be a theater.
Exposed brick. Heating pipes. Out of its era.
Three dressing-room tables for three performers.

The lights take a long time to rise all the way.

DONNY *sits and meditates somewhere. Eyes closed.*
So completely still that you think he is a part of the set.

TRAE *lays on his back on a couch. He tosses a paper ball up and down.*

Someone is playing music through a little speaker.

TRAE. I think it makes me nervous that it doesn't make me nervous anymore.
Do you know what I mean?
Like, okay, I remember you came up to me at the gym. And you said
I like the way you lift.
And I was like
Hey I'm so sorry, mad respect but I don't roll that way.
And you clarified that you weren't, like, coming on to me.
You just wanted to know if I wanted to make some money.
…
And that was three years ago!
I mean you been doing this even longer. How long you been out here for?

TRAE *looks to* DONNY.
DONNY *is meditating.*
TRAE *knows not to interrupt.*

And the first time, you showed me the ropes.
Brought me down here, and walked me through what to expect, what to do if someone is being extra, how to stay composed and Rock Solid.
And it felt very…
Like okay my mom was around. When I was a kid.
And, she had an idea of what love was, and so she loved me.
But sometimes you want love to be… Constructive. And, instructive? Not…

…
And three years ago when you put me in front of my first audience, I was like
Oh shit.
It was terrifying. I was nervous. I was afraid.
Everyone looked so… hungry?
And you told me ahead of time. You warned me. And ultimately, the job is simple.
Just go out there, flap your dick around, listen to the music and see where it takes you.
The dots'll connect themselves.
And it's. You know it's like the first time someone explains sex to you.
My mom gave me the talk when I was in first grade.
But she started with condoms.
Like before we even got to – I didn't even know the word vagina yet!
I didn't know what sex was and she's showing me how to put a condom over my two fingers.
Because she was terrified I would do what everyone else in my family did
and either get pregnant or get someone pregnant at sixteen.
And it's like, because I had this talk, and because I know what a condom is
I'm supposed to know what sex is?
…
…
But then you fuck a few times and I mean the dots do connect!
And so before my first show I was so nervous.
Like this can't be a real job.
Like I just go out there, do some dance moves, let them take my clothes off, and they'll just have their way with me?
…
And we get out there…
And there was this one woman who was so thrilled to be there.
She looked like a kid the first time they watch *Sailor* –

GEOFF. SHAQ ATTACK!!

GEOFF *enters and stuffs the paper ball that* TRAE *was playing with.*

Whaddup whaddup!

GEOFF *is in a bear costume.*

What we talking about? Donny in the zone!

DONNY *doesn't react.*

GEOFF *works out. Fast, intensive movements. Off and on.* TRAE *recovers the piece of paper, unbothered.*

TRAE. I was saying how the first girl I danced with looked like, I don't know, like a kid watching *Sailor Moon* for the first time –

GEOFF. You watched *Sailor Moon*?

TRAE. No! No of course… I mean I remember flipping through the channels as a kid and *Sailor Moon* was on one and I was like whoa…
but then I was like *nah I can't watch this.*

GEOFF. So why is that your example?

TRAE. Aight fuck it no. I mean like. Skittles.
The first girl I danced with looked like a kid having Skittles for the first time.
And it's like OH MY GOD SKITTLES THIS IS FUCKING AWESOME.

TRAE *checks the clock. It's almost showtime. Time to prep.*
He cycles between different static exercises.
Holds a plank as long as he can. Side plank. Yoga.

GEOFF. Ohhhhh Trae had a Bethany.

TRAE. Her name was Bethany?

GEOFF. Nah I'm saying she was a Bethany.
A Bethany. Like. Has fucked but hasn't *been fucked.*
Prolly got a boyfriend or husband. Or wife even.
But hasn't been UHN'd yet. Or UHN'd on demand. On *her* demand. It's different.
Your first party girl was a Bethany.

GEOFF *unzips his bear suit. Begins rubbing his body with oil.*

TRAE. For sure.
And she looked so hungry to play with me.
And I was like, oh… I know how to do this.
And after that. Every time it made me less and less nervous.

GEOFF, *facing away from the audience, begins fluffing himself.*

GEOFF. There's Bethanies. Danielles. SERENAS. Vivicas. Every once in a while a Noah, which is, whatever.

TRAE. Right. And now I'm like, anyone could come in and I'd be fine. I'd be just fine.

GEOFF. Cuz you're a goddamn pro.

GEOFF *is frustrated with himself.*

Aw fuck. I think I'm.
Ay Donny can you take a look at this.

GEOFF *goes over to* DONNY, *who is still meditating.*

Donny am I looking a little small today? Like three-quarter inch off?

DONNY *opens his eyes. Looks at* GEOFF.

DONNY. Full inch.

GEOFF. AW FUCK.
Who got the China pills?

TRAE, *from whatever exercise he's holding, points to his backpack on his table.*

It's too cold in here. Pipes don't do goddamn shit.

DONNY (*still meditating*). We don't control the pipes.

GEOFF *goes to look for a pill.*

TRAE. And I'm saying it doesn't make me nervous anymore.
But it doesn't make me excited either.
And even when I'm fucking my girlfriend.
It's like, she comes so easily with me. And she has many of them. Like back to back to back.
Which is rare, supposedly. Like apparently most women don't come with most men?

GEOFF. We ain't most men heehee.

TRAE. But for her it's like this big, powerful experience. This guttural release –

DONNY. It's The Beast…

Silence.
DONNY *is still meditating.*
TRAE *and* GEOFF *look at* DONNY *to elaborate on 'The Beast.'*

He doesn't.

GEOFF. Cuz good dick is hard to come by.
And so when you get it, you wrestle it down and you fucking bank that shit.
You crucify yourself on that dick.
Trae you're a motherfucking sacrament.
Let that bitch pray! Aw yeah here we go.

GEOFF *finds and pops a pill.*
DONNY *ends his meditation. He costumes up. Ritual.*

You want one?

GEOFF *tosses a pill to* TRAE. TRAE *takes it dry.*

TRAE. No but I'm saying I don't feel anything.
Not excitement. Not nervous. Not love. Love?! Am I supposed to feel love during sex?!
Right now there are like twenty women out there –

DONNY. It's twenty-eight. Twenty-eight covers tonight.

TRAE. Almost thirty women out there.	GEOFF. Big night baybeeeee!

TRAE. Who are paying INCREDIBLE money for something they thought was illegal.
But it's not! God bless the state of New Jersey it's not.
Thirty women out there who I am going to fucking entertain.
And the brave ones are going to get all of my body.
And some of them will discover their bravery by using me.
And I just feel like a. A. A not what used to be there!

DONNY *grabs* TRAE*'s costume bear head.*

And nothing has replaced it. And I miss whatever used to –
Like when you get fucked the way you deserve to be fucked and it makes you feel like a newborn baby like nerves excitement terror
Like this bright big light that my whole life used to be built around.

It's the *Sailor Moon* again!
And *Sailor Moon* is not there anymore and I don't even know what's supposed to be there in its place –

DONNY *moves to* TRAE.

DONNY. Do you come?

TRAE. What?

DONNY. With your girlfriend. Do you come?

TRAE. Most times, yeah.

DONNY *hands* TRAE *his bear head.*
He puts one hand on TRAE*'s shoulder.*

DONNY (*deep*). All things come and go.

DONNY *walks away to get his own bear head.*
TRAE *is like um is that advice useful?*

TRAE. Yeah I don't think that actually answers my –

GEOFF *goes to* TRAE. *Slaps his cheeks and holds his face.*

GEOFF. Hey hey my guy my dude my friend.
I love. I love. I LOVE. When you get all interspective and whatnot.
But yo.
Let's imagine any dude from any where. Call him Bill.

TRAE. Who is Bill?

GEOFF. Bill is Bill he's whatever he's hypothetical he's Bill he's no one.
But then!
Bill suddenly has a tight-ass body.
Bill has a girlfriend whose favorite food is to fuck.
Bill makes his girlfriend come with the brush of his fingers.
Bill makes his living by getting a dozen blowjobs a night from bachelorettes and all he has to do is not ejaculate for sixty minutes plus encore.
Okay.
Bill is not Bill.
Bill is just some dude from somewhere.
You are Bill.
Okay, Trae.

Everyone wants to be Bill and somehow you are Bill.
How fucked is that. That you get to be Bill.
You. YOU!

TRAE. Yeah me.

GEOFF. YEAH YOU!
Now are you gonna get that dick hard or do I have to do it for you.

GEOFF *playfully grabs* TRAE*'s crotch.*
TRAE *twists away.*

Huh! Huh?!

TRAE. Nah nah nah you're right you're right!

GEOFF. Yeah I am!!!

GEOFF *grabs his bear head.*

WOO!!!!!!

DONNY *turns off the music.*
They all meet DONNY *in the center of the room.*

DONNY. Gents.
We've got twenty-eight covers for the night.
A bachelorette party of six. Veronica will be in a tiara. But she's nervous so we let her come to us.

TRAE. Heard.

DONNY. Another bachelorette party of five. Micah will be in a white jumpsuit. Her man is incapable of lifting her in the air so tonight we are gonna make her touch the ceiling.

GEOFF. Love a leg day.

DONNY. Now there is also a DIVORCE party of three.
Tristyn was cheated on by the father of her four kids.

GEOFF. Aw fuck dude.

TRAE. Hate that shit.

DONNY. They were together for… seventeen years…
Despicable. It's really despicable.
Now Tristyn's friends say that she's feeling like her body has

changed a lot since the last time she was single, and she doesn't know how to let somebody new look at her.
So gents.
We find Tristyn and we worship every inch of her body.
We make sure she is always within arm's reach of a hard dick or an asscheek.
We eat whipped cream off of her fingers and let her give us what her ex-husband refused to respect.

GEOFF. Fuck yeah!

DONNY. Someone once told me that if a dream were possible, it wouldn't be a dream.
Well.
Today we go out there and we teach these women that they haven't dreamt big enough.

TRAE. Let's go.

DONNY. We are the dreambreakers.
We are the market.
We have no competition.
No one can do what we do.
If you haven't heard of what we do then you haven't googled the right things.
We are not boy toys; we are MAN TOYS.
We are dancing bears!
WE ARE DANCING BEARS BABY!

TRAE & GEOFF. YEAHHHHHH!

DONNY. HOO!

TRAE & GEOFF. HA!

DONNY. HOO!

TRAE & GEOFF. HA!

DONNY. HOO!

TRAE & GEOFF. HA!

GEOFF (*losing it*). LET'S GO!
LET'S GO BABY!

GEOFF. LET'S GOOOOOO!! TRAE. RAHHHHHHHH!!

At this point, they all have their bear heads on.
DONNY *smacks them both on the ass.*
GEOFF *smacks them both on the ass.*
TRAE *receives the smacks and then, less authoritatively, smacks each of them on the ass.*

They keep smacking each other on the ass and jumping and screaming as they exit the stage into the glowing light of the party room.

The party rages on somewhere we don't see.
The lights go off in the dressing room, but we see the distant party lights.
We hear the muffled bass, distant screams, a setting sun.

The bass cuts out.
The lights calm.

The music quiets to a hum but continues.
A kind of transcendent peace.

Clean sheets.
    Silently watching TV with your mother.
A lover grabbing your pinky with their pinky.
    Eating until you're full.
Sunlight on bare skin.
    Whispering in a crowded room.

When the lights begin to rise again on the back room, DONNY *is alone onstage.*

He sits in front of his old-school desktop computer. The light bouncing off his face. He sits there for quite a while.

He grunts to himself. He is not happy with what he's seeing.

TRAE *enters.*
He puts his bag on his table.
He looks at DONNY.

TRAE. You're not meditating?

DONNY. No I'm not.

TRAE *takes some things out of his bag.*

TRAE. I was thinking about what you said about how all things come and go.
Couldn't sleep last night.
My girlfriend was knocked out and I was holding her.
And I was doing that thing where you try to sync up your inhales and exhales with the person sleeping next to you. So that you're in rhythm and you don't wake them up with your breathing. Do you do that? Ha.
But my mind was just… All things come and go.
And I think that's a valid stance, like, against the backdrop of all of time
but I don't think that's ACTUALLY what I'm experiencing.
I –

DONNY *grunts*.

Everything okay?

DONNY. Hmmmph.

TRAE. What's going on?

DONNY *nods for* TRAE *to come over and look*.
TRAE *stands behind* DONNY.

What, what am I looking at?
Is that…?
It's porn?

DONNY. It's not porn.

TRAE. It's three dudes dancing naked for a crowd of women and.
That's porn.

DONNY. It's not porn.

TRAE. Yeah it…

TRAE *takes a closer look*.

DONNY. 'Wednesdays through Sundays at the Millennium Club. Must call ahead.'

TRAE. Um. That zip code…
Millennium Club that's like.
That's a few blocks away?

DONNY. Yes sir.

TRAE. But… if they're doing this a few blocks away…

DONNY. Mm-hm.

TRAE. I thought we? But I thought we were like?
So there's another group?!
What are they calling themselves?

DONNY. The Dancing Bulls.

TRAE. THE DANCING BULLS!
Does Geoff know about this?
He's gonna lose his –
Does Margie know?!
Ohhhh she's not gonna –

TRAE *walks away.*
TRAE *comes back.*

Oh shit they're really good dancers. They do five nights a week?
Wow and look at that all three of them dance.

DONNY. I don't dance.

DONNY *hasn't taken his eyes off the computer screen.*

TRAE. Jesus.

DONNY *grunts.*

Okay but they're like. We've been doing this for years.
This was posted, couple weeks ago.
So they're newbies. We're landmarks.
They can't mess with OH MY GOD!!!!

TRAE *stands in shock, mouth aghast.*
DONNY *does not flinch.*

TRAE *leans in to get a closer look.*

That's the –

DONNY. Yes.

TRAE. That's the…

DONNY. Yes.

TRAE. That's the biggest dick I've ever seen.

DONNY. Uh-huh.

TRAE. Can you zoom in on that?

DONNY. Don't know how to zoom.

TRAE *leans over and zooms it in.*

TRAE *gasps with his whole body.*

TRAE. We can't let Geoff see this.

TRAE *goes to close the desktop like a laptop.*
DONNY *moves the mouse around in a useless panic.*

You gotta close, you know how Geoff gets if he –

DONNY. How do I get outta full screen –

TRAE. WHO USES A DESKTOP DUDE!

GEOFF *enters.*

TRAE *and* DONNY *both stand and try to act natural.*
TRAE *throws a towel over the desktop.*

GEOFF *goes to his station. Doesn't see them.*
Puts his bag down.
GEOFF *seems very low-energy.*

TRAE *and* DONNY *try to act natural. It's so weird.*

GEOFF *sees them.*

GEOFF. What?

TRAE. What? What who, what nothing.

DONNY *grunts.*

GEOFF. You're being mad weird right now.

TRAE. You're beinggggggggg, why are you being so quiet man what's up what's going on?

GEOFF. I just walked in?

TRAE. The other day you were all Shaq Attack.

GEOFF. Oh so now I can't just enter a room? I can't just go to a place without speaking my everything? Am I allowed to walk into a room I love and just like be myself whatever that self is on any given day –

TRAE. What?

GEOFF. – Or am I just some fucking clownfuck, the fuck man?

TRAE. What the fuck is going on with you?

GEOFF *notices the desktop.*

GEOFF. Why is there a towel over Donny's computer?

TRAE *looks at* DONNY.

TRAE. Yeah man why is there a desktop, towel on your desktop?

DONNY *is frozen.*

DONNY. I was watching porn… And beating it… Beating it vigorously… nearing… completion.

TRAE *looks at* DONNY *like what the fuck are you –*

GEOFF. The fuck are you talking about?

TRAE *face-palm.*
DONNY *is like I did my best.*

GEOFF *slowly moves to the desktop without taking his eyes off of them.*

What am I gonna see on this computer screen?

TRAE. We just have to believe it's gonna be okay.
Pepsi gotta have Coke.
Domino's – Pizza Hut.
Baskin-Robbins – fuckin, fuckin, fuckin –

DONNY. Who eats Baskin-Robbins?

TRAE. Dairy Queen!

DONNY. It's Ben & Jerry's.

GEOFF *snatches the towel off the desktop.*
He looks at the screen.

GEOFF. Oh so you WERE watching porn…

GEOFF *looks closer.*
TRAE *takes a seat.*

What, what is this?
The Millennium Club is this, is that around the corner?

GEOFF *looks at* TRAE *and* DONNY. *They don't look back.*

Uh-huh…

GEOFF *slowly backs away from the computer.*

Then. He very swiftly turns and kicks the shit out of the coffee table in front of TRAE.

TRAE. HOLY SHIT DUDE! DONNY. HO!

TRAE. YOUR ENERGY IS WAY OFF TODAY!

DONNY *goes to restrain* GEOFF.

GEOFF. Does Margie know about this? I can't lose this job man they can't put us out of business!

DONNY. We don't know.

GEOFF *breaks free.*

GEOFF. Nah it doesn't matter.
We got. You know. We got the hogs man.
We got the hogs.
Trae hits them with 8.75.
You whip out the hairy 9.
I finish with anywhere from 9.5 to 10 depending on the temperature outside.
Right? Just say I'm right.

DONNY *looks down and shakes his head like it's worse than you think.*

GEOFF *rushes back to the computer screen.*
He watches.

(*Mortified.*) Aw noooooo.
That's gotta be.

DONNY. Twelves across the board.

GEOFF. THAT'S NOT EVEN PRACTICAL!

TRAE. And all three of them actually dance.

DONNY. I DON'T DANCE. ME NOT DANCING IS. That's not the issue here let's.
Boys we gotta focus!

They herd around the desktop.
Fury. Horror. Curiosity. Wonder.

GEOFF. God the girls are hanging off it like a fucking monkey bar.

DONNY. That's almost fifty covers in there.

TRAE. They're… really good at dancing.

They watch.

Is there volume?

TRAE *turns on the volume.*
We hear a chorus of femme voices, screaming like an amusement park.

GEOFF. Oh I can't hear that I'm gonna puke turn it off.

TRAE *tries to turn it off.*

– Turn it off! Dude turn it –

TRAE. – I'm trying it's a freakin time capsule –

GEOFF. – No the monitor is separate from the speaker –

GEOFF *slams buttons until the whole thing shuts down.*
Quiet.

DONNY. …do you think it saved my tabs?

GEOFF. Does Margie know about this?

TRAE. We haven't heard anything.

GEOFF. She's not gonna, like, fire us and look for different guys is she?

DONNY. I don't know.

TRAE. She's taken care of us since the beginning.

GEOFF (*to* TRAE). Have you ever actually met Margie?

TRAE. No.

GEOFF. Me either.

DONNY. She's a businesswoman. She just wants good business.

TRAE. Well having a neighboring club with hotter guys is not good business.

DONNY. Just because they have bigger dicks does not mean they're hotter.

TRAE. Mmmmmbut they are.

DONNY. Don't say that man.

TRAE. What it's not bad to admit. THEY'RE HOT. They're fucking hot.
And it's okay. People can be hotter than me. Objectively.
That is totally allowed, that –
THEY'RE SO HOT.

GEOFF. This is what always happens. You think you have something good.
Something special. And then…

A long moment.

TRAE. Ya know what? No. No!
Forget these Dancing Bulls and their twelve-inch synchronized dicks.
A Boeing 757 don't mean shit if you can't land it.

DONNY. 757s have one of the worst safety records in modern aviation.

TRAE. Exactly!
And you know what, we have something that they don't have.
We have some goddamn pizzazz. We got that sauce.
And the people know.
So all we gotta do is go out there and do our thing.
The product speaks for itself!
And you know what we are?

TRAE *grabs* GEOFF*'s cheek.*

(*To* GEOFF.) You know what we are?

GEOFF. The product!

TRAE. THE product! The ORIGINAL Dancing Bears.
Donny how many covers we got tonight?

DONNY *gets his clipboard.*

DONNY. We have.
We have ten covers.

A moment.

GEOFF. That's low.

TRAE. That's low, okay yeah that's low.
But we get lower!

TRAE *drops it low.*

(*Dropping it low.*) Yeah. Yeah. This is what they want.
Geoff you gonna get low with me?

GEOFF. Fuck it, where the China pills?

TRAE. What I'm talking about!

GEOFF *goes to take a pill.*

DONNY. Gents. This is actually interesting.

TRAE *gets back up.*

Tonight is a group of women from Jefferson Middle School.
They're all teachers.

TRAE. Aw see? Nobody is more underpaid, more undervalued, than public-school teachers.
Should we give them the Full Lockdown?

GEOFF. Oooh we haven't gotten to do that in a minute.

TRAE. See this is what makes us special.
The Dancing Bulls are just a buncha cocks.
But us? We're a bunch of dicks.

DONNY. Alright. You remember your entrances?

TRAE. We are gonna show these teachers, we are gonna show Margie, we are gonna collect our checks, and we are gonna be the best Dancing Bears this country has ever seen.

TRAE *gathers everyone.*

Shall we?

Blackout.
A flurry of lights. The show is about to begin.

Then.

DONNY *is there. Center-stage.*
Dressed as a hot, gruffy administrator. Clipboard in hand.

His voice is slower. Deeper. Dire.

A crowd of women cheer.

DONNY. Alright settle, settle.
Good evening. My name is Mr Donovan.

WOMEN IN AUDIENCE. Hi Mr Donovan.

DONNY. I see we're excited tonight.
That's good. But.
Save it.
Because we have some serious business to get into.
It's my job to make sure you are prepared.
In case of emergency. Because we live in a very, very dangerous world.
But. The good news is that we have ways of handling the danger.
First thing to know:
There are fire exits there, there, and there.

He points out the fire exits in the theater.

In the event of a fire, we will proceed in a calm manner.
To the nearest exit. Okay?

WOMAN IN THE AUDIENCE. Hi Daddy!

DONNY. That's inappropriate ma'am.

He loves it, but it's hotter not to.

We will move calmly together and meet out on the corner by the blue phone.
And we will check our bodies to make sure no one has been hurt.
Is that understood?

WOMEN IN THE AUDIENCE. Yes sir! / Alright cowboy! / Check my body!

DONNY. Now.
Unfortunately, there are other dangers that we have to be aware of and prepared for.

And I hate to have to do this, but it's just a fact of the world we live in.
I'm going to talk to you now about active shooters.

DONNY *seems like he really hates this truth of the world.*
He rubs his head with his hand.
He slips a hand under his button up and rubs his shoulder, in a stressed way that also reveals part of his chest.
It's really hot.
He's about to make an active shooter training really hot.

Because we live in a scary, scary world.
And I don't want to alarm you.
From the bottom of my heart, there is nothing more that I want
than for this to be a safe world for you ladies.
...
But it's not a safe world. It's a dangerous one.
And it's my job to keep us prepared.

WOMAN IN THE AUDIENCE. Keep us safe Daddy!

DONNY. Ma'am if I have to warn you again, you're in trouble.
Now.
In the event of an active shooter, the first thing to do is run.
Leave your things behind and run.
Getting away is the top priority.
You run like your life depends on it.
But.
Sometimes that doesn't work.

We hear the sudden sound of doors locking, slamming shut.
It's jolting to the guests in the audience.

DONNY *is feeling himself.*

Sometimes you can't run.
So then you hide. Silence your electronic devices and hide.
Don't move a muscle. Don't make a sound. Don't even whisper.
Or else. That's it for you.
But sometimes. Sometimes there aren't enough places to hide.

Another slam.

You've done your best. You've followed all the rules.
You've exhausted all of your options.

Your heart is pounding so hard you think you'll explode.
That's called adrenaline.
It's your body telling you that you want to survive.
Your last resort:
Fight.

Music begins.
A woman shouts.

This is the world we live in.
You are in danger, but you know how to handle danger.
When a masked stranger approaches.

TRAE *and* GEOFF *enter calmly, dressed as bears.*
The audience cheers.

You do not run. You do not hide.
You outnumber them.
Nothing is off-limits.
You use your hands, your mouths, you dig your fingernails into the skin of anything that stands between you and what you desire.

TRAE *and* GEOFF *line up next to* DONNY.

In sync, they all begin unbuttoning their shirts.
One by one.

The women scream.

This is the world we live in. It's dangerous. You could get hurt.
But your body knows what to do.
You fight like you've never fought before.
AND YOU GET
EXACTLY WHAT YOU NEED.

THE MUSIC BOOMS.
THE LIGHTS BOOM.
THE BEARS HAVE UNBUTTONED ALL THE WAY AND UNLEASHED
THREE DICKS SHEATHED IN NEON.
ASSCHEEKS OUT IN JOCKSTRAPS.

ON BEAT, THEY SWING THEIR SHEATHED DICKS LIKE WINDMILLS.
LIKE HYPNOSIS.

THE CROWD GOES CRAZY.

TRAE *and* GEOFF *do a synchronized dance while* DONNY *hypes them up.*

They go into the audience. They grind. They bounce.
TRAE *is acrobatic. He does a backflip. Some breakdancing.*
GEOFF *is classic sexed-down hip-hop.*
DONNY *doesn't dance. He has his own sexy way of interacting with the audience. But it is not dancing.*

If the audience has one-dollar bills, they should be thrown. If they have green paddles, they better wave that shit now. We promised these people a show. Goddamnit we are giving them a show!

At some point, all three of them end up back onstage. They each stand in a spotlight.

Boom. They all do some kind of move/pose.
TRAE *has a little dance solo.*

The audience cheers.

Boom. They all do a different kind of move/pose.
DONNY *has a solo that is not dancing.*

The audience cheers.

Boom. They all do a different kind of move/pose.
GEOFF *has a solo.*
Except, GEOFF*'s move is kind of spastic.*

GEOFF. Aw yeah! Yeah baby! Yeah! Let's go!

GEOFF*'s movements get a little off. A little wild.*
He's body-rolling and humping the air.
He's speeding up. He's not on beat.

Unh. We. Oh god yeah.
Oh yeah.
We. Ha ha. We. We.

GEOFF *is kind of collapsing.*
His bear head falls up.
He's humping the ground.
He's clasping his chest.

TRAE. Uh Geoff?

Something is happening to GEOFF.

DONNY. Hey man, hey are.

GEOFF. Haaaaa. Hernnnnn. Mmmmmmm.

He's sobbing.
He can't stop sobbing.

DONNY. Hey hey hey!

DONNY *goes to* GEOFF *and holds him.*
GEOFF *sobs like a person who has never heard of sobbing, at once hyperventilating but also unsure how he could possibly be experiencing this.*

TRAE *doesn't know what to do.*

Blackout.

The sound shifts.

A kind of transcendent peace. The audience sits in its pulsing light.

Leaving a lover's house to sleep in your own comfier bed.
A fluffy omelet.
Watching the football team you grew up with.
Catching the street lights turning on.
A warm mug in your hands.
Rocking to sleep in your father's car.

Lights slowly rise on the empty back room of a performance club that used to be a theater.
It's quiet onstage for a long moment.

B. *enters.*

B. *has never been in this space before.*
B. *finds it repulsive and intriguing.*
B. *sniffs the air. It smells more pleasant than* B. *thought it would.*

B. *looks at the clipboard on the wall. Studies it. Puts it back.*

B. *checks out each man's station.*
B. *looks at the desktop computer.*
B. *looks at Trae's desk. Picks up a framed picture of Trae and his girlfriend.*

B. *goes to the costume and prop rack. Fire hoses.*
A stethoscope.
She tries on the stethoscope. She knocks it. Ow! She hurts her ears.
It's real.

B. *looks in the hamper. Pulls out a jockstrap. The jock part is… long.*
B. *looks at it, indifferent. Tosses it.*

B. *goes to* GEOFF*'s table.* B. *fishes around, really with no sense of caution or restraint.*
B. *pulls out a long tube attached to a hose. It's like a dick-shaped oxygen mask–*

GEOFF. It's a penis pump.

B. *didn't see* GEOFF *standing there.*
He entered about halfway through B.*'s snooping.*

B. *doesn't quite know what 'penis pump' means.*

GEOFF *briskly takes it from her and pantomimes using it, a demonstration.*

He tosses it back on the table and takes a seat across the room.

Some cock rings in there too.
Pick a ring; let's get married.
Are you Margie?

B. It's cold in here.

GEOFF. That what I –
What I always fuckin say but they act like I'm crazy for being affected by the temperature.
Are you Margie? Are you here to shut us down Margie?

B. You've never met her?

GEOFF. My bank account has.
…
Donny's only one who's seen her in person though.

B. *cracks up. Sighs.*

B. That psycho bitch.
…
You don't think it's inordinary to have never met your boss?

GEOFF. What about this job seems ordinary?

B. *shrugs, indifferent.*

So you're not Margie?

B. I'm her daughter.

B. *goes to light a cigarette.*

GEOFF. Could you not? Donny got asthma.

B. Seriously?

GEOFF *finds his jockstrap outside of the hamper.*

GEOFF. Hey I don't know what you think this is, but just cuz we dance and fuck doesn't mean we're disorganized.

B. *puts the cigarette away.*

B. Margie never mentioned me?

GEOFF. No. But I've never met Margie.

B. Does not surprise me one bit.

GEOFF. I don't mean to be disrespectful.
But uh,
who the fuck is you?

B. Margie sent me.

GEOFF *sighs deeply. The inevitable.*

GEOFF. It's what I thought.

B. I thought there were three of you?
Aren't there three of you?

GEOFF. I'm on laundry today…

GEOFF *goes to the hamper. He stands by it.*
He angrily slams his jockstrap down into the hamper.
The sound was not nearly as dramatic as he thought it'd be.

He picks up the hamper and some detergent and heads out the exit.

(*Leaving.*) Excuse me.

He's gone.
From offstage, we hear GEOFF *put laundry in the machine.*
He kicks the machine a few times.

(*Offstage*.) FUCKKKKKKKKKKK FUCKING FUCK!

Silence.
Some quarters drop into the machine. The machine starts.

B. *pulls out a vape.*
B. *vapes.*

GEOFF *re-enters hastily with the detergent.*

(*To* B.) Hey look I don't know who you are or why Margie sent her daughter of all people, but I assume you're here to be the bearer of bad news and shut us down or fire us or whatever the fuck because the Dancing Bulls are next door and they're putting on what they think is a better show. And they got, they got, you know they got bigger dicks and they use a buncha mousse in their hair. And you're prolly thinking like *oh we can't compete wit that*. And if we talking purely, purely on the basis of girth and length then sure fine though I will say me Trae and Donny are admirable as – we're the cat's pajamas when it comes to that category, and truthfully I've only met three bitches who could take a full ten inches so twelve is a goddamn busted cervix if you ask me, but you're not asking me. You're here to tell me my services are no longer needed and put a bullet in my brain behind the barn. And I'm here to tell you you're wrong because ultimately the point. The point is. The point is:
I love women. I love our audience. And sometimes it's men too and sure I gay for pay but the fact is I'd give my left nut to please em. Take the right one too; hell make it a two-for-one special that's what this is all about. It's not about dicks or muscles or nothing it's how you make em feel. And that's all I wanna do is give em that feeling. That UNH.
And that's special that's. You know. Put an ad in the paper. Go scout the gyms and peep the biggest bulge you can.
I bet you could find a bigger dick. But you NOT gonna find another Geoff.
And I need this job. I don't know your name but I need this job.

A long moment.

B. Are you the one who cried?

Another moment.

GEOFF. Okay what the actual fuck are you here for?

B. *vapes.*

B. I'm B. I'm Margie's daughter.

TRAE *enters.*
He sees GEOFF *and* B.

TRAE. Um. Hi?
(*To* B.) I'm Trae.

B. I'm B. I'm Margie's daughter.

TRAE. Oh fuck. FUCK, okay, okay.
(*He prepares his monologue.*)
Hey I know it's a tough business out here but the fact is we really love women –

B. You're not getting shut down.
Look. My mother
is a woman
full of secrets.
My whole life.
So when you say none of you have ever met her, it comes as no surprise.

TRAE. Donny's met her.

B. Well at least she spends time with one of us.
She and I haven't spoken in… yeah.
Occasionally, she'll send me an email.
Asking for something. Never money. But always something.
And I always fly to the rescue and get pulled in way too deep.
And when I was young, it was because I 'wanted her love.'
And now she's old so it's because 'she's gonna die soon.'

TRAE. Aw hey you don't know that.

GEOFF. AY WHOA SHOW SOME RESPECT.

B. Just a fact. She's my mother, she's older, she's one step closer to death.
It's not a sad thing. It's just. It's nothing.
And so she sent me an email. All caps because she doesn't know how to take it off.
And the email said:

'BULLS TAKING OVER. MEN CRYING. NEED NEW SHOW.'

GEOFF. Okay calling it crying is a stretch.

TRAE *gives him a look.*

B. And so I'm supposed to help you make a new show.

TRAE. Uh… you do know what we do in our shows, right?

B. The Dancing Bear porn thing.

TRAE. But we're not the porn we're the real thing.

B. And some people are into it apparently.

GEOFF. Fuck you mean some people?

B. I mean less than most, more than a few?

GEOFF. Are you kidding me right now, everybody is into it and if they say they're not they're –

B. – Well no but the thing is –

GEOFF. – What you haven't been put on yet? –

B. – I don't think there's anything to be put on to –

DONNY *enters.*
Looks at everyone.

GEOFF. Ay Donny. This lady is supposed to give us a new show.

A moment. DONNY *looks at* B.

DONNY. You look just like your mother.

DONNY *goes to put his things down.*

B. Well now that's a stretch –

GEOFF. Donny you hear me? She's trying to give us a new show.

DONNY. Already have a show.

B. See but you don't.

DONNY *stops.*

Yeah um. It turns out panic attacks and Dancing Bulls are not good for business.

You're right about that.
And so Margie cancelled your shows for the next couple weeks.
Like when a restaurant has a cockroach outbreak and they close up / to fumigate –

GEOFF. I / told you she's shutting us down!

B. And also because we're not renting a space and running a show for an audience of four – you're not shut down –

TRAE. It was more than four – GEOFF. Who is 'we?!'

DONNY. Was going downhill.

B. You can look at the clipboard you had four tonight, five tomorrow, and one on Saturday.

GEOFF. ONE? ON A SATURDAY?!

TRAE *grabs the clipboard off the wall.*

B. And so yeah so. It's kind of up to me now to determine when we / reopen –

GEOFF. Who is we?!

B. Because I guess excuse me I guess my mother also is sort of grooming me
to take over the business?
Which is not my business but also you know me daughter to the rescue, as I explained.
But I am sort of your boss now. So.
Roaches.
Fumigator.

TRAE. She's right.
(*The clipboard.*) It's…

GEOFF. Wow. Okay don't shut me down, just kill me, just SHOTTY TO THE FOREHEAD –

TRAE. Extreme –

GEOFF. BLOWN BRAINS ON THE MOTEL CEILING –

B. I'm sorry you cried.

A moment.

Panic attacks can be really, really scary.
Especially if you don't know that you're having one.
I've had them and it makes you feel like your inner skin is revolting against itself.
It's okay. It happens. And this is a space where we can talk about it.

A longer moment.

GEOFF (*to* DONNY). Now what in the fuck / is this?

B. Oh my god I was trying to empathize and –

GEOFF. What kind of therapy ass –

TRAE (*to* B.). We try not to really talk about it.

B. Oh sorry I assumed it was your favorite topic.

DONNY (*to* B.). What do you do for a living?

A moment.

B. I'm a sculptor.
I don't know.
I used to be a sculptor. I went to school for it.
And then.
I wanted to be a counselor –

DONNY. Counselor?

B. Because the artist-to-therapist pipeline is.
Went to school for that.
Hated it. Clients were dumb.
And then I thought librarian for some reason.
Because books.
But it turns out that also requires more school.

GEOFF. Where you get the money for all that school?

B. …Margie.

GEOFF. And where ya mama get her money from?
…
Ol' woo-woo ass, I could've gone to school.

TRAE. No you wouldn't have.

GEOFF. What!

DONNY. When do we reopen?

B. I suppose 'when I say so.'
…
When there's a new show.

DONNY *takes off his hoodie. Gets loose.*

DONNY. Alright.
I guess we've got some work to do.

A moment.

TRAE *joins* DONNY.

GEOFF *is like WHAT THE FUCK?*

GEOFF. WHAT THE –

Blackout.

There's no peace here.

Lights up.

DONNY *appears to be meditating again.*

B. *sits on the couch going through papers.*

TRAE *and* GEOFF *watch her warily.*

B. This is illegal.

DONNY. It's not.

B. *looks to* TRAE *and* GEOFF. *They shrug. They look at* DONNY. DONNY *is meditating.*

B. I don't know anything about the law –

GEOFF. No you didn't go to law school too?

B. But how does this not violate, I don't know, every prostitution law?

GEOFF. Cuz I ain't a hoe.

TRAE. Geoff yes you are. By every definition you are.

GEOFF. Yeah but it's different.

TRAE (*to* B.). The way Donny broke it down to me, and he can come out of meditation if I mess it up: around the time internet porn got big, there was this this subcategory of porn called 'Dancing Bears.' Are you familiar?

B. Enlighten me.

TRAE. Basically, a couple hot dudes would entertain a dozen or so women, civilians, in a club. Like a strip show, the men were the performers and the women were the customers. But they'd go one step further; they'd make their whole bodies available. So it's male strippers plus, you know, the women can grab, touch, lick. And these dudes would be hard for so long, really impressive stuff. And as the video progresses, eventually one of the women would just kinda grab a dick and stick it in. Like full penetration, right? And it was this SUPER popular genre. With like, what were the sites?

GEOFF. Bangbros, FapStation, RedTube, 89.com, the works. You not familiar with them either?

B. FapStation?

GEOFF. She doesn't even know the classics!

GEOFF *scoffs*.

TRAE. And most people thought the content was real. But it wasn't. Everyone was a paid actor. But the companies know that viewers love the idea of amateur videos. Same deal with casting couches. Content where theoretically normal people are having sex like, with pure abandon. Sounds nice right?

B. If that's your thing.

TRAE. And this is where, I guess where your mom comes in? Because she realized that if the fantasy was there and people believed it was real then the market must be there too. Like someone must be googling '*Are Dancing Bears real?*' So she, I guess, found Donny. And this club grew from that. The Real Dancing Bears.

B. Based on porn?

GEOFF. There's the porn and then there's the real thing. We're the real thing, based on the porn.

B. Once again, I must ask: HOW IS THIS LEGAL AND HOW DID MARGIE MAKE THIS HAPPEN?

TRAE. Well, the party girls take fake names.

B. Do you?

TRAE. No Trae is my government. Travis. And… wait Geoff do –

GEOFF. Geoff. All me.

TRAE. Yeah so just the girls. They pay to secure their spot. And then two documents: we sign an NDA, and they sign a release to film the evening. So technically we're making art for art's sake. But the NDA restricts us from ever releasing it, not that we'd ever intended to. But for legal purposes, we're just making a very very specific form of art that is only to be experienced but never seen outside of this room. Not legal in many places, but legal in Jersey. Also in Vegas, Florida, and LA. If you ever decide to watch porn and that warning flashes in the beginning of the video and there are those numbers and codes at the bottom. Google those codes, it's all spelled out.

A moment. B. *processes.*

B. Wait so you have all these women on tape?

TRAE. Technically yeah I guess. Hard drive somewhere. But just as a legal, what, deterrent. We're bound to never release them.

Another moment.

B. HOW THE FUCK DID MARGIE FIGURE THIS OUT?

DONNY. Because your mother is a smart woman.

DONNY *emerges from his meditation.*

Feel free to ask more questions, but I for one would like to work.

B. Sure, let's. No wait sorry. I just. I don't get who your audience is.

GEOFF. Whaddya mean you don't? Why are you confused, Trae told you: the chicks come through, they get worshipped en-goddamn-masse and then they leave mindblown or whatever.

B. Sure but how do you keep getting customers? Like it just seems like a niche kink. I mean no tea no shade I'm sure the fetish community is out there –

GEOFF. Yeah yeah yeah stop with the fetish and kink PC lingo, it's not –
What we do is about women. Okay.
That's all.
Have you ever had sex with a woman?

Everyone looks at B.

B. Give me an NDA too and I'll answer questions.

GEOFF (*mocking*). omigodNDAhahafuckoff.
I don't care who you rail.
Here's a truth: women have this secret personality that comes out when they fuck.
It's true. Trae and Donny will both agree.
Donny?

DONNY. The Beast.

GEOFF. Uh-huh.
Trae, your girl?

TRAE. Oh yeah, when we fuck she goes full I don't know, it's almost so personal I can't even watch.
I don't even know what's happening usually. Certainly doesn't happen to me ha.
Kind of an exorcism? Like she's being exorcised from the inside out?

GEOFF. Possession, carnivore, primal animal call it what you will.
When a girl gets fucked the way she deserves to get fucked, it's sickening. It's special.
It's gross.
And ya know, I'm not ashamed to admit that women have closer friendships than men.

TRAE. Aw man I don't know about –

GEOFF. Nah nah nah lemme make my point. Cuz see, these women come here with their best friends, their bridesmaids, 'the girlies.' And none of them have ever seen what their friend's animal looks like. I mean how many people have

seen their closest friends have an orgasm? Maybe the world'd be a better place. I don't know.
So they come as a group. And they watch us. And they fuck around with us.
But mostly they watch each other watching us. Watch us please their friends.
And they're like, oh whoa, that's how my best friend of twelve years sucks a dick.
Oh man I didn't know my childhood sis could make that noise.
Wow I thought I knew my maid of honor better than anyone, and somehow I didn't know that she had this in her.
And now I know!
Okay?
Because I have seen the faces of women after our shows, as they exit the theater.
They've got nirvana in their eyes.
Their lives, their friendships, forever altered.
That train ride home won't make a lick of sense.
Do you know what I'm saying?

A moment.

B. Hmm.

GEOFF. Hmm what?

B. Well. It can't be that special if you're being replaced by another crew with slightly bigger dicks.

GEOFF. OH COME ON!

B. That's not a judgment, that's just, like, what is happening.

GEOFF. Fuck that.

B. Isn't that why I'm here? They have bigger dicks / so clearly you aren't THAT –

GEOFF. Trae get the chair.

TRAE. Is that necessary?

GEOFF. Boss bitch is still confused.
Trae get the chair; Donny hit the Bluetooth.

DONNY. Wait how do I do that again?

GEOFF. Jesus okay Donny you get the chair. Trae get the Bluetooth.

B. What's this now?

GEOFF. No no you're done asking questions.
Donny you said you wanted to work.
Let's work then.

DONNY *grabs a chair. Places it center-stage.*

DONNY. Geoff's right.
Can't know us till you've seen us.

GEOFF (*to* B.). Margie brought you in to take over and you don't know shit.
(*Mocking.*) *Oh I went to college, oh I have DEGREES, oh my mama owns the business.*
Bitch please. You have nothing to offer.
Sit in the chair.

B. Are you serious?

GEOFF. What did I say about questions? Some things only exist between bodies.
Trae where's the music!

B. Oh careful I don't want you to have another panic attack.

GEOFF. A-HA-HA-HA-HA get –

GEOFF *physically moves* B. *with the ease of a man who can toss a woman around, and places* B. *in the chair.*

TRAE *connects to Bluetooth. Plays some music softly.*
A slower song than the last show. Something more old-school.

B. Should I act impressed?

GEOFF. You don't need to act at all.
Trae get her.

TRAE. You want me to go first?

DONNY *and* GEOFF *look at* TRAE.
TRAE *looks at* B.
B. *crosses her legs.* B. *looks insultingly unimpressed.*

Actually, B. *looks one step beyond that.*
B. *looks completely stoic.*
Evaluating from a place that is utterly inaccessible.
B.*'s face does not change.*

TRAE *reads this expression as a challenge.*
Challenge accepted.

TRAE *moves to* B. *as if to seduce.*
He starts slow. Working his way around B.*'s chair.*
Like a bird of paradise. Ritual. Sleek. All for B.
The youngest brother who lives to prove himself.

B. *does not move her body or her eyes. Only her head.*
Expressionless.
Following TRAE*'s every move. Evaluating.*

TRAE *gets more intense. Impressive.*
Spinning on his knees, stopping on a dime.

He finishes his routine.

GEOFF. Do you get it now B.?

B. *makes eye contact with* GEOFF.
Nothing.

TRAE *tags in* DONNY.

DONNY*'s routine is more like a lion playing with his food.*
He opens by ripping his shirt in one smooth motion.
He runs his hand down the front of B.*'s body without touching.*
He never touches B.

His routine is all squats and Adonis.
Begging B. *to admire his form.*
Coming as close to B. *as possible.*
Musk and pheromone.
Distance and prey.
Withholding as a father.

If he can, he lifts B. *and the chair in one motion.*

B. *has watched every motion.* B. *has not flinched.*

DONNY *saunters away from* B.
Finished with his routine, like a big cat leaving the animal who plays dead.

Without hesitation, GEOFF *tags himself in.*

There's no other way to say it: GEOFF *is pure sex.*

GEOFF *touches* B.
Sliding through B.*'s legs.*
Bringing B.*'s hands up his own legs.*
Nuzzling his head up B.*'s torso.*
Eye-contact all the way.
The older brother whose attention you bask in.

He pulls B.*'s chair down so that* B. *is on the ground.*
He crawls over B.*'s body.*
69-ing the air around B.

In one motion, GEOFF *lifts* B. *into the air and bounces her on his pelvis.*
He lays B. *softly on the ground.*

That was the cue.

TRAE *and* DONNY *join* GEOFF.
They give B. *the full special.*

Three men praising all of B.
Moving B. *into various positions.*
Rolling like acrobats on a playground.

If this was sex, B. *would have been tossed into at least five positions*
in the span of sixty seconds.

Cowgirl.
Reverse Cowgirl.
Sideways.
The Other Sideways.
Standing Upside-Down 69.
Bulgarian Split.
Mounted Python.
Downward Dog.

In the chaos, B. *stands up.*

B. *walks over to* TRAE*'s phone.*
B. *disconnects the Bluetooth.*
B. *shuts the music off.*

Quiet.

GEOFF, TRAE, *and* DONNY *are all heaving, out of breath.*
B. *is fine.*

B. *looks at each of the men, their heaving chests, their sweat, their exhaustion.*

Finally, B. *makes an expression. A noise.*

A chuckle. It grows. It spreads into a laugh.
A full-body laugh. B. *can't control it.*
B. *is laughing so hard.*

The men join B.*'s laughter, confused.*
Mistaking B.*'s laughter for pleasure.*

This makes B. *laugh even harder.*
It becomes clear that B. *is laughing at the men.*

B. *can barely stand.*

The men go silent. They look at each other.

B. *pulls herself together.*

B. Sorry I just –

TRAE. Did we hurt you?

B. *looks at the men.*
B. *busts into laughter again.*

B. Your faces! I'm sorry. I. I'm trying to figure out if I should say the thing I'm thinking.
(*To herself.*) Should I say it? Oh man I'm gonna break your little hearts.
I'll say it. I'm gonna say it.
Yeah I'm gonna say it.
Well yeah okay so.

B. *takes a moment.*
Then, deadly serious.

Nonc of you are men.

A moment.

GEOFF. Uh. What?

B. Wow yeah. Sorry.
I don't know why I'm saying sorry, I'm not sorry.
Oh man.
OH MAN. I mean that colloquially by the way. Not referring to you.
No yeah wow.

It's so clear to me.
(*To* TRAE.) You are not a man.
(*To* GEOFF.) You are not a man.

GEOFF. I don't know who you think you are but –

B (*to* DONNY). You are not a man.
Wow this is maybe the most clarity I've ever –

GEOFF. No sexless bitch / is gonna pop up in here and talk shit to my face –

TRAE. Ay Geoff –

GEOFF. No no don't tell me nothing –

B. Why are you like this?

GEOFF. I'll slap my dick on the table right now talking bout some not a man bitch what are you –

B. I asked you a question!

A moment.

GEOFF. Say it again?

B. Why are you like this?

GEOFF. I don't understand.

B. I'm aware.
Wow.
Oh wow.
There is simply so much work to do.
…
Let me rephrase: who told you this was attractive?
…
Who told you this was attractive and why did you believe them?

A moment.

GEOFF. What… what do you mean?…
The whole world? All of history?
Every girl I've ever – what do you mean who told me.
Do you know how much what we just did for you would cost on a Saturday night?
Sex. Beauty. This shit is craft!

B. I didn't find it beautiful.

GEOFF. You wouldn't know beauty if it kicked you in the clit.

B. *laughs.*

B (*to herself*). Margie you madwoman.
…
Okay. Yeah okay.
I'll do it.

TRAE. You'll do what?

B. Donny do you have the tapes of your past shows?

DONNY *nods.*

Can you give them to me?

DONNY. I think the whole thing is that I can't share –

B. Sure. But I won't, no one will see, Scout's honor.

DONNY. And… I don't know how to get them off my desktop…

B. But I can watch?

DONNY *shrugs.*

Okay.
Well, yeah so, okay.
We've established that none of you are men.

GEOFF. Say that again and –

DONNY *puts a firm hand on* GEOFF*'s shoulder.*

DONNY. Control.

B. We're going to fix your show.

B. *goes expressionless again.*
B. *goes to sit in front of* DONNY*'s desktop.* B. *turns it on.*

The men watch, unsure what's happening.

(*Without looking at them.*) You can leave.
I'll see you tomorrow.

The men look at each other.

Oh and Geoff?
Call me a bitch one more time and I'll rip your nose off.

Blackout.

Except for the light of the computer screen, flashing on B.*'s face.*

B. *watches tapes.*
B. *watches tapes.*
B. *watches tapes.*

Lights up.

TRAE *is seated on the couch, holding a teddy bear.*
DONNY *is seated nearby with a notebook and pencil.*

GEOFF *a bit further away.*

There are kids' toys scattered about.

B. *spins her chair around and faces the men.*

You're doing well, Trae.

TRAE. How do you know I'm doing well?

B. Donny, he's doing well, right?

DONNY. I can show you my notes?

TRAE. Really? I feel like I…
Okay. Um.
Yeah so usually what happens.
She and I will have sex most days, at least once.
Usually I'm pretty tired, but we both work weird hours.
So I guess we're both tired? Doesn't matter.
And, I read somewhere that fifty percent of couples have sex less than once a week?

DONNY. Is that true?

GEOFF. How do you have sex less than once?

TRAE. It's like, statistics.

GEOFF. Yeah I know what statistics are.

B. It's true.

GEOFF. Fuckin low.

B. Don't judge.

GEOFF. 'None of you are men' isn't a judgment?

B. Can we let Trae talk?

TRAE. So I guess.
I don't know why this feels weird right now.

B. Where do you start?

TRAE. Um.
I guess we kiss.

B. Where?

TRAE. What do you mean where?

B. I imagine there are a lot of places one could –

TRAE. Right, sorry.
The lips.

B. Fast or slow? You can use your words.

TRAE. Um. It depends how we get into it.
But usually slow.
And I clasp my hands around her cheeks.
My wrists go under her jaw, so it's sort of like she can put the whole weight of her head into my hands.
And she goes a little weak in the knees, but that's the point.
Because I can hold her up.
And then I bite her bottom lip. And lean back. So that, I guess it feels like I'm holding her, moving her with just my lips.
And then I move her face out of the way with my hands.
So that I can start working on her neck with my tongue?
And I follow the muscles of her neck. The veins. It sounds scary.
I suppose it is. If I were a wolf, this is how I'd strike.
And I think she likes that, because this is usually where she smiles.
I love that part. I can like hear her smile.
And while my mouth is going, my hands are squeezing her…

B. Ass?

TRAE. Yeah. Sorry it felt wrong to curse.
And I lift her onto me. She wraps her legs around my waist.
If there's a wall nearby, I slam her against it
but I keep one hand around the back of her head so that her head doesn't hit the wall.
And… I hold her up with my pelvis. So that my hands are free.
And I can take her shirt off.

TRAE *looks to* B. *for permission to keep going.*
B. *gives it.*
As TRAE *speaks, he slowly relaxes. Disappears in and out of his memory.*

And so her shirt is off.
And I run my tongue from her neck to her nipples.
It feels like I'm there for hours.
And she feels like she's floating. Like I can feel her skin turn into goosebumps.
This is usually where she tells me how wet she is.
And so I throw her onto the nearest surface.
And rip off her, you know, her pants, her panties.
And I run my nose from her ankles to her crotch.
Between her legs.
But I don't touch her. I just hover there.
Breathing on it. Taking her in. And it's like I can smell her whole day.
Where she's coming from. Where she wants to go.
I can smell how wet she is.
I stay there until she's shaking.

GEOFF *raises his hand.*
B. *acknowledges* GEOFF.

B. Geoff?

GEOFF. I'm hard.

TRAE. Dude. DONNY. LET THE MAN FINISH.

B. No it's okay.
Geoff, would you like to talk about your erection?

GEOFF. What? No I'm joking I'm not, I'm lightening the mood – JESUS YOU ARE NO FUN.

B. Alright then. Trae you can continue.

TRAE. Um.
Sorry no Geoff is right this is starting to feel weird.

DONNY. OH COME ON!

B. Wait no Trae we were really getting somewhere.

TRAE. What do you mean? How are we getting somewhere I don't even know where we're going.

B. I think it'll be best for everyone if you finish your story.

TRAE *takes a moment. The vibe is off now.*

TRAE. Yeah so I don't know. I eat her out, she usually comes twice.
On the second time, I start fucking her while she's coming so that she keeps coming.
I toss her around. She has some kind of crazy exorcism demon orgasm.
And then when I get the sense that she's too tired to move, I try to come.
And then I pull out and come on her stomach because she's not on the pill.
And yeah we usually fuck like every day, every other day.
Does that cover everything?
Are you still fucking hard Geoff?

TRAE *throws a pillow at* GEOFF.

GEOFF. Ow dude not when you tell the story like that I'm not.

TRAE. Because you killed the vibe.

GEOFF. What vibe? What are we even doing here?

B. I'm making a point.

TRAE. What point?

B. Trae, would you describe yourself as 'good at sex?'

TRAE. Um. I feel like that's not up to me to decide?

DONNY. I would describe him as good at sex.

TRAE. What?

DONNY. Hypothetically.

B. Trae your modesty is so interesting. Have your past partners described you as good at sex?

TRAE. Yeah, I guess yeah, across the board, yeah.

B. How did you get good at sex?

TRAE. I just wanted to be?

B. Try harder.

TRAE. What?

B. Give me a better answer.

TRAE. How?

B. You mean to tell me as a kid you had dreams of being good at sex?

TRAE. Actually yeah.

B (*surprised*). Really?

TRAE. Yeah.
Like I remember watching sitcoms. *The King of Queens. My Wife and Kids. Everybody Loves Raymond.*
And the running joke was always that husbands were terrible at sex.
No foreplay. They'd come in thirty seconds. Fall asleep instantly.
And the wives were always upset.
And so I was like okay. In order to be good at sex, I have to be like the opposite of these dudes. I can't come quickly.
I have to love foreplay. Whatever I do, I can't –
Like I used to jack off and practice holding it for as long as I could.

GEOFF. Holy shit I did the same thing!

TRAE. Yeah dude.
I mean it was to the point where, I wouldn't even come with girls usually.
Like for the first four years of my sex life, I never came once.

GEOFF. Ever?!

TRAE. Homie no! Not from sex, from head, nothing!
Which made me feel fucking crazy because my whole life I had heard that men came so fast.
And I was all the way on the other side of the spectrum and I never came.
It was so psycho. My partners didn't complain, but I felt insane!!

GEOFF. Yo how have we never talked about this?!

TRAE. I don't know!!! It was so crazy!

GEOFF. So wild.

TRAE. I was like am I gay?
Is it gay if I can't come with women?

GEOFF. Wait no / that doesn't mean…

TRAE. I even tried watching some like gay porn – but that did nothing for me.
And then I finally came with this girl Diane and I was like ohhhhh okay ha!
…
But yeah so I guess I've always been good at sex.
…
…

GEOFF. Wait it's not gay to not come… right?

TRAE. No!

GEOFF. Right no right?

TRAE. Right.

GEOFF. Yeah yeah.

DONNY. I always come.

TRAE. Yeah but you're a tank.

DONNY. Talkin buckets of paint. Renovate your apartment.

GEOFF. Aw Jesus dude yeah this is how I know I'm straight.

B. Trae I'm going to ask you one more question.

TRAE. Yeah sure?

B. Do you enjoy your sex life?

TRAE. …I don't understand.

A moment.

B. I can say it again if you want.
…
Do you enjoy your sex life?

TRAE. Um. My girlfriend is beautiful?

B. You did hear my question, right?

TRAE (*growing frustrated*). No no I heard I just feel like I'm answering.

B. You're not.

TRAE. And I've been in the spotlight this whole –

B. It's my last question I promise.

TRAE. And I answered, I described in brutal detail –

B. Why is this a hard question?

DONNY. 'I don't feel anything.'

A moment.

'Not excitement. Not nervous. Not love.'

B. What's that?

DONNY. That's you.
That's Trae.

TRAE. You some kind of human tape recorder?

DONNY. You think I'm not listening when I meditate.
I remember everything.
…
You said it not me.

TRAE. Yeah but I meant like… Donny I don't even know why you're bringing that up –
Of course I like sex.
I.
(*Losing it a bit.*)
You know I think I mentioned this but this whole thing is starting to feel weird and pointless. I have answered every single, and I don't know why I'm the one being picked on but B. it's actually really dawning on me that you are a COMPLETE stranger and I'd really love to know what your point is –

B. I'll / tell you –

GEOFF. THAT'S / WHAT I'VE BEEN SAYING THIS WHOLE TIME!
WHAT DOES SHE KNOW!

TRAE. Because it's actually not normal to just divulge all of this to –
Exactly what do you know! Respectfully –

B. It's not a 'yes or no' question it's an explanation if you're gonna ask me a question sit the fuck down and lemme give you an answer!
...
Yesterday, I stayed here and watched hours and hours of footage from your shows.
I stayed overnight. I didn't sleep.
I just watched. So many different shows. So many women.
And now.
...
Now I'd like to talk to you about the imaginative failure of straight male pleasure.

GEOFF. This bitch!

B. Yes I think –

B. *stops*. B. *realizes that* GEOFF *just called her a bitch again*.
B. *considers*.

She doesn't really have a choice, does she?

B. *very calmly walks up to* GEOFF.
B. *sticks two fingers up each of* GEOFF*'s nostrils*.
B. *twists* GEOFF *down to the ground by the nose*.

GEOFF *screams*.

B. *drags* GEOFF *by the nose*.
B. *throws* GEOFF *by the nose onto the ground*.

Not quite ripping his nose off, but definitely making a point.
GEOFF *holds his nose*.

GEOFF. WHAT THE FUCK WAS THAT?

DONNY. I mean she did warn you.

B. I'd like to talk to you about the imaginative failure of straight male pleasure.
...
Trae I've asked you some questions but I think I already knew the answers.
And to answer the question that you wouldn't: no, you don't enjoy your sex life.

Everyone looks to TRAE.
TRAE *is silent.*
B. *is feeling herself.*

You don't love it because you don't know what pleasure is.
None of you do.
You live your life based on an idea of pleasure.
I remember sitting in intro to figure sculpting, and learning about the male figure.
Dates all the way back to the Greeks. The same tools and the same techniques.
The particulars of how to sculpt the muscles and sinew.
What to do with a chisel!
And I was terrible at it because it was just an idea.
And here are you three.
You're not real men because you're just an idea.
I realized this when I watched you dance.
You're performing patriarchy.

TRAE. Because that's what the women want?

B. I don't think that's true either.

DONNY. Um –

B. I mean obviously it is in some ways.
But that's why you're so replaceable.
Because you're trying to be an idea that is not your own.
Trae, your sex life is empty because everything you do is for your girlfriend.

TRAE. Um. I don't…
She really, really loves when we have sex.
It's like, what we're best at. Like, without it I don't know what we'd…
She told me it's the best sex of her life.
And I love it when she comes.

B. But don't you think that's limiting? Your sense of pleasure comes entirely from being inside of someone else's pleasure.
…
I mean you said it yourself. You got good at sex by trying to not be the male archetype you saw on screen. But just because you're trying to be a better idea doesn't mean you're not just an idea.

TRAE. But. I think you're not taking into account how much I really, I really love making her happy.

B. And does she feel the same way about you?
Or does she just assume that you love it because you're a man?

TRAE. Well. I mean.
I don't know, I'm the one doing the fucking.

B. And what a shame. You could give a thousand women a thousand orgasms
and never once know how to articulate your own pleasure.

Oh shit.
B. *is on a roll.*

None of you are real men because your masculinity is unoriginal.
An easy sculpture.
And so you're being replaced by some sculptures that are slightly better than you.
And you can't do anything about it because they are right.
You don't know anything about yourselves; you just know what to present to women.
Not to toot toot. But yeah actually.
Patriarchy isn't good for men either. Oppressive systems don't equal joy for the oppressor.
They equal safety. And safety is boring. It is ugly. It is cliché.
So now I am asking you: what is risky masculinity?
Who are you?
Why are you?
And how do we make your show something that is so uniquely you
that no Dancing Bull could ever touch it?

A long moment.

GEOFF *raises his hand.*

Yes?

GEOFF. My nose is bleeding.

GEOFF*'s nose is bleeding.*
B. *gets him some tissues.*

DONNY. And this will be sexy?

B. shrugs.

B. I don't know.
But… does this make sense?
Am I crazy? Tell me if I am.
Trae does any of this resonate with you?
…Trae?

TRAE *has disappeared into himself. His head in his hands. Then, suddenly.*

TRAE *lets out a single whimper from somewhere inside of him. Somewhere that hasn't been touched until now.*

It echoes into a blackout.

Skipping rocks alone.
Wiping the dust off of a plant's leaves alone.
Cleaning your kitchen alone.
Doing laundry alone.
Having the best sleep of your life alone.

The lights slowly come back.

B. *watches as* TRAE *and* GEOFF *do a slow movement exercise where they try to match each other's movements without leading or touching.*

It starts slow, but eventually morphs into something quite confusing and beautiful.

DONNY *sits far away with his notebook. He watches. Jots things down.*

B (*to* DONNY). The exercise works better if you participate too.
Use the toys as inspiration.

DONNY. I don't dance.

B. Does this look like dancing to you?
…
Have you ever danced?

DONNY. I don't dance.
And so I don't dance.

B. But how can you participate?

DONNY. I am participating.
Look at them.

B. *looks back at* TRAE *and* GEOFF, *who are now both standing closely.*
Looking into each other's eyes.
Practicing stillness.

B. *moves to them.*

B. Yes this is good. See how it feels to –

GEOFF *leans in and pecks* TRAE *on the lips.*

TRAE. Aw dude what the fuck.

GEOFF (*cracking up*). Heeheeheehee.

B. Guys.

GEOFF. What, we're dreamily staring into each other's eyes how could we not?

TRAE. That's, like, ruining the exercise.

B. No actually why don't we get into it.
Geoff, I think we should talk about your homoerotic tendencies.

GEOFF. Homorotic?
What about this is homorotic?

A moment.

B. Are you asking me what about two men kissing is –

GEOFF. You're telling me that's gay? Psh that's not –
I'll make out with him right now.

TRAE. No you won't.

GEOFF. Fuck you say?

B. No I encourage, if you want to explore –

GEOFF (*to* TRAE). You think I wouldn't?

TRAE (*a challenge*). I think you wouldn't.

GEOFF. Boy I will split your cheeks and put you through the goddamn headboard.

TRAE. Geoff no you wouldn't.
If anything, I mean, I would ruin your life.

GEOFF. Oh you would ruin my life?

TRAE. I would, I would ruin your life.

GEOFF. B. who you think would ruin whose life?

B. I –

GEOFF. Boy I ruin lives as a hobby.
I would blow your goddamn cheeks out.
You couldn't run. You couldn't walk.
Every single step you took, you'd be thinking about how deep inside of you I was
How you almost grasped the hand of God –

TRAE. I just don't think so –

GEOFF. Motherfuck I'll tear that ass up you give me a good five minutes.

TRAE. See but it wouldn't even take me five minutes so I just don't know what we're talking about here.

A moment.

TRAE *and* GEOFF *both look at* B.

B. So there is definitely some tension –

GEOFF. I actually don't think this is that confusing or that gay.
I'm just saying that hypothetically if me and Trae fucked,
I would be the best fuck of his life.

TRAE. And I'm saying that that is simply not possible.
Because I would be the best fuck of HIS life.

GEOFF. And I'm happy to let you believe that and be wrong.
Because unhypothetically, I love pussy.
That's the truest thing of all.
(*To* TRAE.) Oh super-soft lips by the way.

TRAE. Oh thanks man do you know Rosebud Chapstick?

GEOFF. Is that like the Ordinary?

TRAE. Nah Sephora. Been on it a couple times a day for a few years.

GEOFF. Oh shit dude.

TRAE. Yeah man it's moist as hell.

GEOFF. I love it. Oh nice dick too by the way.

TRAE. What?

GEOFF *ball-taps* TRAE.
TRAE *keels over.*

Fuck you got me.

A moment.

B. *is actually quite stumped here.*

DONNY. I'd like to be in the hot seat.

Everyone looks at DONNY.

DONNY *stands.*
DONNY *moves to the 'hot seat,'*
which is just the seat where TRAE *was.*

TRAE *moves out of* DONNY*'s way, still in pain.*

B. I just want to clarify that it's not a hot seat.

GEOFF. Oh shit Donny in the hot seat!

DONNY *sits.*
He is in a zone. Not looking at anyone.

They gather nearby.

Just warn us if you gonna let out a moan like Trae did.

TRAE. Fuck you I couldn't help it.

B. Again, this is not a hot seat. I don't want to create pressure. That being said, Donny I would love if you could talk about why you don't dance.

DONNY (*avoiding eye contact*). No.

B. …no as in… hello?… no as in I won't talk about why I don't dance… or no as in –

DONNY *opens his notebook.*
He reads.

DONNY. I remember the names of every woman I've slept with, and what it felt like when they came.

A moment.

DONNY *is not a natural reader.*
The notebook looks tiny in his hands.
DONNY *continues.*

I watch from above like a boy with a magnifying glass.
Elizabeth came and it turned her whole body into a shudder.
Layla came and her arms flailed like wings.
Natalia came and her toes flexed like a ballerina on pointe.
Caroline faked it at first, and then Caroline came like it surprised even her. Like she wanted to fight it and the fight made it more uncontrollable.
Sam came like a child asking for one more snack.
Sheria came and clung on to my body like a starfish.
Emma came and cried and apologized.
Rubana came in waves that never stopped, and she hated me for it.
Holly came and her whole body smiled.
Steph came like a teacup in my hands.
Natasha came so hard I couldn't stay inside of her.
Alicen came and her whole body contorted. Something ugly leaving her, something else finally breathing.
…
I've always been afraid one day my daughter would meet someone like me
and make all the same mistakes her mother did.
…
That someone would ruin her the way I've ruined people.
I'm afraid I've closed doors for her.
I'm afraid my existence has left a hole that can never be filled.
I don't know what is better. To love and hurt.
Or to never feel it at all.
…
I don't think anyone will ever remember me the way that I remember them.

DONNY *looks at that last sentence for some time*
like he can't believe he wrote it.
He closes his notebook.

Everyone is staring at him.

GEOFF. Holy fuck dude…
…
…

B. Donny…

GEOFF. YOU HAVE A DAUGHTER?!

DONNY *doesn't move.*

TRAE. I didn't know you had a kid…

GEOFF. How many years we been working with each other,
how did I not know you had a kid?
That's like big life shit.
How did –

B. Wait nobody knew you had a child?

DONNY. Because.

GEOFF. Cuz what? See this is what the fuck I was saying about male friendship yo what the hell.

DONNY. Because it was… bad.
I was bad. With.
Her mother. And…
I haven't seen or talked to her since she was three.

TRAE. How old is she now?

DONNY *does some math.*

DONNY. Twenty-four.

A moment.

GEOFF. Twenty-four.
…
Holy shit you have a twenty-four-year-old.
That's like, that's a full-ass adult.
You have a full-ass adult?!

B. And so you just don't talk to your daughter?

DONNY *shakes his head no.*

A moment.

What the fuck is wrong with you?

Everyone turns to B.

Something different is coming out of B. *right now.*
A nerve.

Do you know where she is?

DONNY. I don't.

B. Do you know how she is?
Do you know anything about her?

DONNY. I find her pages sometimes.

B. Her pages?

DONNY. Facebook. Instagram.
She graduated college.

B. Oh okay! She graduated college well that's a fact must be all good then!

TRAE. Um B. –

B. No. Sorry. But. I'm not sorry. Twenty-one years!
Why don't you talk to her? Is there a reason?

DONNY. I don't I, I, uh, I –

B. Or are you just another cowardly parent who's afraid of their child.

DONNY. It's better.
For her and her mother if they don't know me.

B. Bullshit. That is such –
This is what you all do.
And then you just pretend we don't exist? Like oops
I exploded a kid into the world,
oh well they'll be fine.

DONNY (*agitated*). It's better.

B. What do you answer when someone asks if you have kids?

DONNY. Nobody asks.

B. That can't be true.

DONNY. Nobody. Asks.

B. Do you know how fucking weird it is to walk into a room and everyone knows your mom but no one knows you exist?

TRAE. Wait I don't know your mom?

DONNY. B. are we talking about my daughter or –

B. 'My daughter' can you even use that phrase? She's not your anything.

DONNY. I wanted to be in the hot seat so I could talk.
Because it's… hard. And I thought maybe… if I wrote
I could… it's hard.

B. It's not hard.
It's hard for us.
For you, no.
Being a coward is not hard.
And if it's so hard then maybe you shouldn't have had us in the first place!

TRAE. Hey maybe we should talk about sex again –

DONNY (*to* B.). You're probably right. Maybe she should've never been born. Maybe I should've never been born.

B. Oh I'm right that's even worse!

GEOFF. Ay chill he's trying.

B. No this is not trying.
This is –
It's you. It's Margie.
And suddenly it's like why am I here.
Why do I even exist if –

DONNY. She is good. I was not good.
She deserves to know people who are good.

B. Well here's a fact: if the last time you saw her she was three then she probably doesn't even remember what you look like.
So.
You're right.
No one will remember you the way you remember them.
…
Congrats. The seat is hot now.

B. *storms out.*

Lights click out.
Something painful in this space.

Realizing you don't like your favorite childhood lunch anymore.
Taking the bows out of your hair for the last time.
Broken curfew.
Your hometown is too small.
Please don't touch me.

Lights slowly rise.

GEOFF *is alone in the space.*
He has headphones on.
We can hear the music through his headphones.
Something like D'Angelo.

He is dancing to his own choreography.
He dances with a focus so innate,
it almost looks apathetic.
He is dead in the eyes, save for the occasional smirk.
A mean mug that breaks through.
Almost as if it hurts him to be this good.
So nice it stings, and he must contain it.
Smooth as water and for no one else but himself.

When the choreo is finished, he restarts.

B. *enters and watches, silently.*

In the middle of the choreo, GEOFF *turns and sees* B.
GEOFF *stops. Takes off the headphones and goes to work at his station.*

GEOFF. Really fucking harsh with Donny yesterday.

B. I know.

GEOFF *keeps working.*
B. *comes closer. Takes a seat by* GEOFF.

What are you doing?

GEOFF. What does it look like I'm doing? I'm sewing.
Trae asked me to make him some shit. Whatever.

B. You sew your own costumes?

GEOFF. What the fuck is your problem?

B. Um what… the fuck is your problem?

A moment.
GEOFF *keeps sewing.*
B. *watches.*

GEOFF. I know you think I don't take you and your shit seriously.
But I do.

B. Oh you do?

GEOFF. Yeah I do.

B. You take me seriously?

GEOFF. I take you very seriously.
I think you don't take us seriously.

B. Oh that's it.

GEOFF. Yeah that's it. That's the nail on the goddamn –
Where are my fabric scissors?

GEOFF *goes to look for scissors.*

You come in here with all your let's explore, let's talk, let's discover our own pleasure.
But some things only exist between bodies.
And I don't think you take seriously how much we like to –
I don't think you understand the pleasure of pleasing.

B. You think I don't understand –

GEOFF. I don't think; I know.

A moment.

B. Okay.
Make me understand.

GEOFF *stops looking for scissors.*

GEOFF. You want me to make you understand?

B. Yeah.
Make. Me.

A moment.

GEOFF. I want you to take your tongue.
And run it along the inside of your cheek.
Feel all over the inside of your cheek.
Do you feel how smooth and cool and wet that is?
Now imagine that
slipping like a warm glove
over the most sensitive part of your body?
And imagine that the more of you that you put inside, the softer and wetter it gets.
That's what it's like for me to be inside of you.
And I think you need to take that seriously.

A moment.

B. And what makes you think you know so much about pleasure?

GEOFF. Because I've been in more pussy than you can imagine.
And I don't try to make it more complicated than it is.
Because it's very, very simple.

A moment.

B. Do you have a girlfriend?

GEOFF. Absolutely not.

B. But you love physically pleasing women?

GEOFF. Like breathing.

B. Do you please them emotionally?

GEOFF. Here we go.

GEOFF *finds his scissors.*

B. Simple question.

GEOFF. Irrelevant.

B. So everyone you've ever fucked, you've only fucked them once?

GEOFF. No of course not.

B. So you have regulars?

GEOFF. Yeah I have people who I keep, who I stay with.

B. Is that so?

GEOFF. Nah don't give me that look, of course I do.

B. Who?

GEOFF. I'm not Donny; you not getting no names out of me.

B. How long?

GEOFF. I have a girl, we've been fucking a few times a week usually, on and off.

B. For how long?

GEOFF. I don't know. Like seven years.

B. You've been in a relationship for seven years?!

GEOFF. Absolutely not.

B. Sure sounds like a relationship.

GEOFF. I promise you it's not.

B. So you have the ability to sleep with a woman for seven years and not consider it a relationship?

GEOFF. Yup.

B. Wow what do you like about her?

GEOFF. Nothing.

B. Do you like her laugh?

GEOFF. It's horrendous, like yours.

B. Do you like her smile?

GEOFF. Nope.

B. Does she have good taste?

GEOFF. Only one thing I taste.

B. Do you hate women?

GEOFF. Love em.

B. I get quite intrigued when people don't answer questions.

GEOFF. That's your choice.

B. If you love them so much, why can't you name a single thing that you like about her?

GEOFF. No reason to.

B. You really can't give a woman a compliment?

GEOFF. Too many words.

B. How often do you have panic attacks?

GEOFF. Not that often.

B. Once a year? Once a month?
Every day?

GEOFF. I can tell you the one place I've never panicked.

B. Yes please tell me I want you to talk.

A moment.

GEOFF. Do you know what the problem is?

B. With you or with me?

GEOFF. With society.

B. I have a feeling you're about to say.

GEOFF. We talk too much. Not everything needs words.
After we fuck, I don't care.
I don't care.
And I know that sounds fucking callous or whatever whatever, but it's not callous.
It's goddamn liberation. To say that's it.
We know what just happened inside of our bodies and NOTHING we say
will come close to that. It is simply, it is, it is simply,
the only thing that we could possibly say is THANK YOU.
THANK YOU FOR TRUSTING ME WITH YOUR PLEASURE.
Now go the fuck to sleep.

A moment.

B. And you don't think we need to explore –

GEOFF. I don't think we need to explore!
I don't think we need to know why.
And honestly, if I have another panic attack then fuck me
I had another.

I know plenty of therapized Lexapro-hoes, and those bitches are still anxious wrecks.
If it's okay for them to be them, it is okay for me to be me.
Now do you have a counter-argument?
Aight then.

GEOFF *focusses on sewing.*
GEOFF *stops.*
He holds his nose out to B.

B. What are you doing?

GEOFF. I said bitch again. If you wanna take another swipe at my nose.

B. *doesn't.*

Suit yourself.
Pass me that bobbin.

B. *does.*

B. The thing that makes us human is language.

GEOFF. Well.
I just watched Donny try really hard to use his words.
For you.
And you eviscerated him.
…
So maybe we should just be silent animals who fuck and eat and beat the shit out of each other. Because I have never heard an animal say I love you or I'm sorry.
And life goes on.

A long moment.
The sound of the sewing machine.

B. I've never had sex.

GEOFF *stops sewing.*

GEOFF. I FUCKING KNEW IT!

B. It's true.

GEOFF. OH MY FUCKING WOW.

B. Yeah go off.

GEOFF. Well well well so the shoe's on the other cock.
See I knew it I can always tell when people are sexless.
You've never fucked?

B. No.

GEOFF. Never sucked?

B. No.

GEOFF. Never kissed?

B. No.

GEOFF. Oh so you a sexual?

B. A what?

GEOFF. A sexual.

B. Asexual?

GEOFF. Yeah are you a sexual?

B. I don't think so.

GEOFF. You sound like it.

B. Mmm no. That word doesn't feel like me.

GEOFF. Wow the nerve of you to tell us about pleasure when you've never experienced pleasure yourself.

B. Well now that part is untrue.

GEOFF. Nah you ain't never had no orgasm.

B. I bet I've had as many as you.

GEOFF. AHHHHHHHHHAHAHAHAHAHA –

B. Are you done?

GEOFF. I just can't believe you'd say that.
Okay. So you…

GEOFF *does a gesture to imply masturbation.*

You, finger all up in there?

B. Nope.

GEOFF *is confused.*

GEOFF. Vibrator?

B. I don't have to touch myself at all.

GEOFF. I don't get it.

B. I'm sure you don't.

GEOFF. Are you gonna enlighten me or just sit there all withholding?

B. I…
Have this place that I go to inside of myself.
I've always been able to go there.
I think even since I was a kid. I remember feeling this way when I was six.
This planet I can visit whenever I please, and it's mine.
It's my planet.
It's like the apex of imagination and beauty. The center of the universe.
Inside of me.
And I close my eyes, my eyes HAVE to be closed and…
…
I just…
I have never seen anything as breathtaking…
…
And I just come over and over and over again.
At home. On airplanes. Whenever I want.
And there is nothing that will ever come close.

A moment.

GEOFF. Nah that's bullshit that's not real.

B. It's the realest thing I've ever felt.

GEOFF. But that's because you've never experienced anything real.

B. It would only be disappointing.

GEOFF. How?!

B. Because that's what disappointment is.
The distance between my imagination and my reality.
Is all disappointment.
I've never seen anything that…
Nothing is more beautiful in reality than in your head.

GEOFF takes this in.

GEOFF. Do it.

B. What?

GEOFF. Right now. Do it.

B. You're not serious.

GEOFF. I told you. I take you so seriously.

B. You want me to come for you?

GEOFF. I want you to prove it.
Prove that this is real.

B. Okay.

B. wheels her chair away.
B. closes her eyes.

B. disappears into herself.
Her mouth opens slightly.
She is on another planet.
Somewhere only B. would recognize.
Memories and sensation that could only be physical and internal.
The smell of rain in the backyard.
Your mother's garden.
The carpet on the staircase.
Bacon sizzling.
A song you loved
but will never know by
name.
Colder water from the bathroom sink.
A pillow between the knees.
The fan turning.
Waking up safe.

B.'s orgasm is so interior you might mistake it for small.
It's not.
It's less accessible.
But it is undeniable and enviable and shattering.

B. opens her eyes. She looks at GEOFF.
For a small second, B. might be embarrassed.
Not ashamed.

Just unsure, as if GEOFF *could almost see where* B. *was. Almost.*

GEOFF. That was it, huh?

B. It's why I couldn't make art.
Nothing I could create in real life could even come close to…
…
…

GEOFF. Thank you for trusting me with your pleasure.

B. I didn't trust you with my pleasure.

GEOFF. No…

A moment.
A deep, unspeakable privacy.
Someone has to break it.

I lost my virginity when I was eleven.

B. Are you serious?
…
I mean Geoff that might explain a –

GEOFF. Shhhh.
Okay.
Not everything is a dot that connects to another dot.
I like who I am. A lot.
Do you?

A moment.

It's funny that you have to have your eyes closed.

B. Why is that funny?

GEOFF *laughs.*

No why is that funny?

GEOFF. It's a control thing, right?

B. That's not the word I'd use.

GEOFF. Trae and I joke about which one of us would ruin the other's life.
And that's fun.

But what I know for sure:
Any of us could ruin yours.

A moment.

B. You wouldn't ever get the chance.

Lights out.

Silence.

We hear:

Dial tone.
Dial tone.
Dial tone.

AUTOMATED VOICE. Your call has been forwarded to an automated voice message system.

MARGIE'S VOICE. It's Margie.

AUTOMATED VOICE. Is not available. At the tone please record your message.

Tone.

A moment.

B.'S VOICE. Mom.
...I know you don't like the phone...
...I can't remember the last time I heard your actual voice...
...I think you don't like me a lot... sometimes...
...But then I think sometimes you know exactly who I am...
...I don't think we're gonna make the kind of show you'd approve of...
...But it's gonna be a show alright...
...I think I'll learn to like me before you learn to like me...
...And the men are probably gonna keep crying.

Lights up.

DONNY *and* GEOFF *and* B.
They are waiting.

B. *paces.*

B. Where's Trae?

GEOFF. No idea.

DONNY. B.

B. What's up?

DONNY. Margie gave me a message for you.

B. She talked to you?

DONNY. Mm-hm.

B. What'd she say?

DONNY. She said.
One week.

B. Oh well that's great that's fucking.
WHERE'S –

TRAE *kicks open the door.*
He saunters in.

They watch him.

He does a weird little dance like he's running the show.
He's on top of the world.

GEOFF. The hell is this?

TRAE. I did it.

GEOFF. You did what?

TRAE. I dumped Alyssa.

TRAE *does a gesture like he's slapping something on a table.*

DONNY. You what?

TRAE. Broke up with my girlfriend.
She's packing her things as we speak.
She's OUTTA here baby!

TRAE *goes to his desk and dramatically throws out the framed photo of him and Alyssa.*

GEOFF. Ay whoa you've been together for like four years.

TRAE. Four and a half and not a day more!
I did just like you said B.

B. Trae that is not what I said –

TRAE. Because I was thinking. I feel like that's all I do is think.
Think about what Donny says. Think about what Geoff says.
Think about what you said.
And you really nailed it when you said
'*limiting*.'
And I thought that is exactly right that is –
Limiting.
I was so limited inside of this relationship. So limited
I couldn't even see it myself
until YOU pointed it out to me.
Because she had no idea how good she had it.
And you were so right.
I was coasting
I was doing whatever she wanted, bending over backwards,
making her come
hundreds and hundreds of times,
and what did I get?

B. Trae –

TRAE. And actually here's the thing:
She, women, straight women, do not understand how much work it is to have sex.
I have to get hard, stay hard, stay inside, hold her, move her, carry her, fuck not too hard not too slow, be exactly in tune with her without her saying a word, I have to be able to blindly navigate all the folds and fleshy curtains of her body WITH MY TONGUE, I have to hurt her just enough to be exciting but not enough to diminish pleasure, I'm still hard by the way I have to stay hard, I have to reassure every single anxiety she might have about herself using just my body, my hardness, the pressure my god the pressure, I have to give and give and give and I mean have you ever, B. have you ever practiced the motion of sex –

B. Trae –

TRAE. No really do it, thrust your pelvis over and over and again
Go like

TRAE *thrusts his pelvis rapidly.*

UHN UHN BLOW MY BACK OUT BLOW MY BACK OUT.
Do it and see if you can keep it up longer than thirty seconds before you get winded,

OH AND BY THE WAY
If you are winded, your dick goes soft so I can't get winded! So it's breath control too! Nobody ever talks about how important breath control is!

DONNY. True.

TRAE. And so I am regulating my breathing, my dick, my tongue, my hands, my weight, YOUR weight, your whole body, not to mention knowing the right time to pull out so I don't wreck both our lives, I am WORKING SO FUCKING HARD, and doing this NIGHTLY
and you just ASSUME
that I should be good at this, that I can do this on a dime, that I should just be able to rock your world and you don't have to know how to rock mine,
that you don't have to know anything about my pleasure because Oh I'm A Man I'm A Hard Dick I Come Quick And Fall Asleep Dicks Are Easy I'm Ray Romano I'm Homer Simpson I'm Jerry Seinfeld
When I Am Just As Complicated As You Are!
And the only reward I get is for you to say:
Wow that's the best sex ever
YOU'RE FUCKING RIGHT.
I AM THE BEST SEX EVER.
FOR YOU.
AND WHAT ARE YOU? BECAUSE YOU ARE NOT THE BEST SEX EVER FOR ME.
THE ONLY WAY FOR YOU TO BE THE BEST
IS IF YOU FUCKED ME THE WAY I FUCK YOU
AND YOU CANNOT DO THAT.
YOU HAVE NEITHER THE TOOLS NOR THE BILLABLE HOURS.
YOU ARE JUST THE FUCKING VESSEL
And you love it.
You love being the vessel as long as I use you right,
and I have spent my entire life trying to earn the ability to use you right
and now I have it, and my hands are empty, and my dick is tired.
I DUMPED HER SELFISH ASS AND GOOD RIDDANCE!

GEOFF. Trae!

TRAE. What!

A moment.
GEOFF *is trying really hard to say the right words in the best way.*

GEOFF. You love fucking her.

A long, long moment.

TRAE. Oh god what have I done.

GEOFF. Hey man. DONNY. Be at peace.

TRAE (*nearly crying*). Oh god what have I done.
I'm freaking out man.

TRAE *crumples.*

GEOFF. Bro it's okay you can get her back.

TRAE. I don't want her back!
Oh god oh god oh god oh god.

DONNY. All things come and go.

TRAE. Stop saying that I don't know what that means.
(*Falling apart.*)
Fuck dude I just wanna be free. I just wanna be free.

GEOFF. Ay man feel it out feel it out –

TRAE. Why is it so hard? Why is this all so hard?

GEOFF. Yeah man.

TRAE (*to* B.). It's your fault!
…
…
…
B. I think you're ruining our lives.

B. I just want to be very clear.
Trae I never said to break up with your girlfriend.
If anything, I just encouraged you to explore.

TRAE. You said I don't know anything about myself.

B. Well –

TRAE. You said I'm a cliché. You said I'm unoriginal and worthless.

B. I did not say worthless –

TRAE. You said what I do cannot be good enough.
You said the way I love is limiting.

B. And you just said you wanted to be free; I want you to be free too!

TRAE. And Donny tried to be, and you –

B. That was a mistake –

TRAE. No it's not a mistake B.
I think this is who you are, really. At your core.
I think you love what you're putting us through.
And I don't even know why –

GEOFF. B.'s never had sex.

A moment.

GEOFF *looks away.*
B. *is furious that* GEOFF *revealed this now.*

TRAE (*teary disbelief*). What?!

DONNY. Is that true?

B. I don't understand why that matters.

TRAE. Oh my god I feel so betrayed. I'm gonna puke.

B. How did I betray you?

TRAE. Because.
You made us vulnerable.
And. You don't know what that's like.

B. I…
Geoff you just saw me –

GEOFF. I don't know what I saw.
Whatever it was, you didn't let me into it.

B. How would I even…
…
…
Sex is not the only way to be vulnerable.

GEOFF. It's a very specific way to be vulnerable.

A moment.

B. Do you want me to go?

TRAE. B. you've given us a lot to think about.
And I think.
I think maybe we can figure out the show on our own from here.

B. But –

TRAE. I used to feel nothing. And, it worked.
And I just don't like. I don't like this feeling.
And I never felt it until you came around.

B. *looks to* TRAE.
Then to DONNY.
Then to GEOFF, *who looks away.*

B. *heads for the door.*

B. *turns back. A ball of contained fury.*

B. I understand that very recently you're all feeling things you maybe haven't felt before.
And I understand that that is scary.
But if you think it is hard for you to feel this feeling.
Imagine how hard it is for everyone else to…
…

B. *leaves.*

The lights slowly fade.

AUTOMATED VOICE. Your call has been forwarded to an automated voice message system.

MARGIE'S VOICE. It's Margie.

AUTOMATED VOICE. Is not available. At the tone please record your message.

Tone.

A moment.
A moment.
A moment.

Tone.

Lights up.

After some time, B. *enters.*

B. *is now intimately familiar with this back room of a performance club that used to be a theater.*

She enters with a trash bag and begins picking up the children's toys.

DONNY *enters and watches.*

B. I took a counseling class once where they suggested that seeing stuffed animals made people more prone to letting their inner child come out. That's why I put these everywhere.
Thought it might make us all…
…
I'll be out of here shortly.

DONNY. I fucked your mom.

B. *stops.*

B. What?

DONNY. Mm-hm.

B. What… what do you mean?

DONNY *calmly goes over to the desktop computer.*
He googles something.
A video plays.

We hear what sounds like a seventies porn soundtrack.

We hear DONNY*'s grunts mixed with a woman's moans.*

B. *comes over to watch.*

That's my mom?!

DONNY. That's Margie.

The moans get louder.

B. Oh my god.

They watch in silence for a bit.

DONNY. She's faking it here for the camera.

B. How can you tell?

DONNY. Much different in real life.

B. You two, outside of –

DONNY. Mm-hm.
Wasn't a big deal.
I mean it was but.
It was more like we were two great friends.

B. Wait but…
How long ago was this?
Because, I've never known who my dad is… and…

DONNY. I've done the math; I'm not your dad.
…
Be crazy if I was though.

B. Can you imagine? You gave me a lapdance…

DONNY. Dark.
…
But yeah so. Your mom was a porn star.
We met on a set.
It was the most normal thing in the world.

B. Was she a good porn star?

DONNY. Why do you talk about her in the past tense?

B. Because she doesn't talk to me?
I don't know.
I'll maybe get a happy birthday email.
I don't even know where she lives.

DONNY. Me either.

B. But she calls you?

DONNY. Every once in a while we talk.
She handles some business stuff.
This whole thing was her idea.
And it's really.
Did you know that in the Great Depression, the only two businesses that turned profit?
Speakeasies and burlesque joints.
Maybe the one thing we always needed.

…
You don't think it's weird to watch me fuck your mom on a computer screen?

B. No. I mean it's more of her than I've seen… ever.
It actually makes me kind of…
…
God this is so weird to say –

DONNY. Jealous?

B. Yeah.

DONNY. Hm. Seems fine to me.

B. How come she never talked about me?

DONNY. This is going to sound awful.
And I don't mean for it to sound awful.
There are some people who simply should not have children.
And then suddenly they have children.
And they think about them every day while also trying not to think about them every day.
And for them, that space is just where they have to live until the day they die.

A moment.

B. Can you tell me about my mom? Like, sexually.

DONNY *laughs.*

I don't know! I'm her daughter and I don't know her.
There's a way that you know her that
is clearly a big part of her.
And a big part of me too
even if I've never…

DONNY. She was terrible at sex.

B. Really?
…
She doesn't look terrible.

DONNY. This is acting.
In real life.
Worst fuck of my life.

B. *cracks up.*

She'd come in ten seconds and then collapse like a rock.
I used to just finish myself off after she fell asleep.
Couldn't move her if I tried. Out cold.

B. Did you hate it?

DONNY. Eh.
Made me feel powerful. Even though it had nothing to do with me.
But that's Margie.
She came like the wind.
…
…
…
I'm sorry.

B. Why are you saying sorry?

DONNY. Because.
Saying sorry to you feels like saying sorry to my daughter.

B. Why don't you apologize to her?

DONNY. …
It was bad. With her mother. I used to… yell.
And, a lot more. Just like my dad.
Tried to lock it down. Just, Rock Solid. Head down. Don't feel too big.
Because if I lose control…

B. What happens if you lose control?

DONNY. I know what happens when I lose control.
My daughter's mother knows too.
And so.
…

B. And so the only solution was to leave?

DONNY. Sometimes you have to do something bad so that you don't do something worse.

B. *takes that in.*
In a way, talking to DONNY *is like hearing from her mother.*

I think we are going to be able to figure out our show.
Me, Geoff, and Trae.

B. Do you think?

DONNY. Yeah. I.
Yeah.
Trae figured out his thing right after you left.
And I think Geoff is almost there too. It's kind of experimental.
And I'm… I'm close.

B. Really?

DONNY. Close.

B. That's good.

DONNY. Hope so.
Might still go out of business. But.
You should come.

B. Oh I probably shouldn't.
I feel like things get… volatile.
I think you've got it from here.

DONNY. Yeah. Well.
Think we got some good stuff.

DONNY *winks at* B.

B. *takes it in.*

B. *gathers the bag of kids' toys and heads for the door.*

B. *has one last thing to say.*

B. Donny I think you are capable of so much.
And yes, we hurt people. We do irreparable years of damage.
And we should do what it takes to earn our forgiveness.
We should!
But you can only punish and deny yourself for so long.
At a certain point, you have to make space for something new.
That's all I want for any of us.
To make space for something new.
Okay?

B. *nods to* DONNY.
B. *goes.*

DONNY *is still for a moment.*

Just as he breathes in –

Blackout.

We hear the sound of a crowd.
It sounds like exactly as many people are in the theatre.

Anticipation.
Anticipation.
Anticipation.

The show is about to begin.
Similar to their first performance.

The doors to the theater open.

B. *enters.*
B. *scoots past everyone and takes a seat right in the center of the house.*

Then.

Lights up.

DONNY *is there onstage.*

The crowd cheers!

DONNY. Alright settle, settle.
Good evening. My name is Mr Donovan.

WOMEN IN AUDIENCE. Hi Mr Donovan.

DONNY. Well hello there ma'am.

WOMEN IN AUDIENCE. Woo!

DONNY. Alright.
Folks. We've got some serious business to attend to tonight.
Now as you may have seen, the Dancing Bears had to take a little hiatus.
To re-evaluate and evolve.
And figure out how better to um.
Deliver the goods.

ANOTHER WOMAN IN AUDIENCE. Hi Daddy!

DONNY. Ma'am... you can do that as long as you like.

CROWD. Woo!

DONNY. Now what you are about to see is the new and improved Dancing Bears.
We had to go on a long, long journey.
And honestly, I don't know where it led.
It's very possible that this is the last show we will ever put on.
Because this business is impossible.
And somehow, through it, we find something very personal and unique.
And we have to share it with you. We have to.
And frankly, hopefully, no one can do it like us.
Because what matters right now is.
Pleasure.

CROWD. Woo baby!

DONNY. Our pleasure.
Your pleasure.
Can we find it?
I said can we find it?

CROWD. OH YEAH / WOO / FUCK YEAH!

DONNY. Your performers today will be Mr Trae and Mr Geoff.
Please welcome Mr Trae!

APPLAUSE! APPLAUSE! APPLAUSE!

Quiet.

Nobody comes.

Hmm.
I'm sorry everyone. It seems like Mr Trae might be feeling a little nervous.
Full disclosure: he just went through a break-up that uh unlocked a lot of things for him.
And so this is a big moment. Let me just –

DONNY *runs backstage. We hear him having a little argument with* TRAE.

DONNY *runs back.*

It's unclear if this is real or an act.
But it works.

Folks. It seems I was correct. Mr Trae is a bit nervous.
And he confessed to me that one of his dreams is…

One of his childhood dreams is for a big crowd to chant his name.
Because that almost never happens to people.
And I think that might really mean a lot to him.
So can we…
Trae! Trae! Trae! Trae! Trae! Trae! Trae!

CROWD. Trae! Trae! Trae! Trae! Trae!

The lights go down.

Music plays.

The crowd cheers.

SUDDENLY THERE IS TRAE
DRESSED IN A SAILOR MOON *OUTFIT.*
THIS IS WHAT GEOFF *HAS BEEN SEWING.*
WIG AND ALL.

WHAT PROCEEDS IS THE SEXIEST, FREEST SOLO DANCE ROUTINE
TRAE *HAS EVER DONE!*

IT INVOLVES GLITTER!
IT INVOLVES PIROUETTES!
IT INVOLVES TRAP REMIXES OF ANIME THEMES!
IT IS SEXY!
IT IS FREE!
IT CARES NOT FOR THE BOUNDARIES OF ANYTHING!

IT IS DEEPLY MASCULINE AND ROOTED IN A SELFISH AND GENEROUS PLEASURE! TRAE *DANCES FOR HIMSELF EVEN THOUGH HE LOVES THE AUDIENCE!*

To put it simply: TRAE *has wanted to do this ever since he was a child*
and so he does it. And I don't care what you call it.

It's TRAE.

TRAE *finishes. His wig is lopsided. His clothing has torn.*

He is smiling.

The crowd goes mad.

TRAE *stands up.*

TRAE (*to audience*). Thank you for trusting me with your pleasure.

In this moment, it becomes clear that this new show isn't perfectly rehearsed.

TRAE *doesn't know which way he is supposed to exit. And* GEOFF *doesn't know his cue to enter.*

They figure it out and TRAE *leaves.*

GEOFF *enters.*

GEOFF. Hey everyone. Whoa that's a lot of people.
Um.
I'm Geoff. Mr Geoff. I'm Geoff.
God this shit is fucking weird.
Oh man I can hardly see y'all.
Can we –

GEOFF *signals to get better light.*

Thanks!
Um.
Okay this section I'm supposed to.
Oh fuck I forgot –

TRAE *runs back onstage still in costume and sets a single chair up for* GEOFF.

Thanks man.

TRAE. Gotchu bro.

TRAE *waves and exits.*

GEOFF (*to audience*). Yeah so. I think you should still have those paddles.
The chair. Um. I'm gonna do some stuff with this chair.
If you are willing and able and would like to be a part of this, raise your green paddle and I'll call on one of you.

People in the audience should raise their green paddles.

Okay yeah you. Yeah don't be nervous. I promise you won't have to do a thing.

GEOFF *helps a member of the audience onstage.*

GEOFF *sits her in a chair.*

Theoretically, this is the set-up for a lapdance.

But.

Oh shit don't we need two chairs?

DONNY *runs onstage and sets up a second chair across from the first.*

Thanks man.

DONNY. Always.

DONNY *waves and exits.*

GEOFF. Okay yeah so.

The lights go down until they are just on GEOFF *and the audience member.*
It is very intimate.

GEOFF *sits across from her.*

GEOFF *improvises some version of:*

Hi. What's your name?
I'm Geoff.
So um.
This maybe isn't going exactly how you thought?
Yeah. So someone told me very recently that I seem to not be able to give compliments.
And so I was like fuck that isn't true.
But then I thought about it and was like oh man. It might… yeah I don't know.
Maybe I should practice giving compliments.
So there's a way that I think I just want to tell you that, I'm just meeting you, but I just want to tell you that you're really, really. Beautiful.
And I don't mean that in any weird way I'm sorry
I know this probably feels like in this moment this is more for me than it is for you
And maybe it is. But I want you to enjoy this too and that's fine if you're not.
It can just be a story you tell your friends.
But for my sake, I think I couldn't live with myself if I didn't tell you that you are drop-dead shoot-me-in-the-back-of-the-neck gorgeous.

And it's annoying that it stresses me out to offer that like
I feel like I shouldn't be nervous right now
Sorry can we hold hands, it's okay if not.
I really didn't – my prompt was just '*Give an honest compliment*' and I'm like how the fuck.
I just think what I'm learning is that I do actually have a lot of… love and…
generosity inside of me.
And I think it's hard for people to know what you think if you don't say it.
I've always just like trusted my body. And I still do.
Like my body can talk about so many things that words could never…
This is so silly.
I just think I am obsessed with your eyes right now.
And the edges of your lips.
And just the fact that you're here I'm really happy that you're here thank you for coming to our show oh my god it's like really big for us that you even came to our show tonight!
…
I think the reason I have panic attacks is because there's something inside of me trying to come out.
And I think we all have something inside of us trying to come out.
And I think that I don't give compliments because sometimes when I give one and look at a person I just kind of, cry a little bit. I don't know why.
I don't know where it comes from… But I kind of like that I don't know.
I think if I had a bunch of words all the time I would…
I have this bigness inside of me that words can't…
And I feel like I can kind of tell that you've also been through things that
have stuck with you too and there's a lot behind there. And. It makes me think.

GEOFF *thinks*. GEOFF *laughs*. GEOFF *tears up a little bit*.

You're really, really beautiful.
And I don't know why it's hard for me to say; that's a me thing.
But I think we're probably never gonna get to do this show again.

And we are so lucky that you are here.
So.
Thank you. For trusting me with your pleasure.

If the person is comfortable, GEOFF *gives them a really big hug.*
They go back to their seat.

GEOFF *pulls himself together.*

(*To audience.*) Oh god okay did I do it?!

TRAE (*offstage*). Woo let's go Geoff!

TRAE *and* DONNY *both enter and give* GEOFF *a hug.*

GEOFF. Yeah yeah aight get off me.

DONNY. Now folks. We know this has not been the show you've expected.
But I think it was probably the show that we needed.
Now. Is this the same thing as us getting naked and slapping our junk around.
No.
No it is not.
Is this harder?

TRAE. Oh my god.

GEOFF. Yo never again.

DONNY. But hopefully it gets easier each time.

A moment.

And with that we'd like to wish you a good –

GEOFF. Donny.

DONNY. What?

TRAE. There's no way you get out of this.

DONNY *deflates.*
DONNY *looks around.*

DONNY (*terrified*). I… I don't know what might happen.

GEOFF. That's okay.

DONNY. You're not gonna make –

TRAE. Mm-hm.

DONNY. But. Um. I think um.
I don't want to scare anyone.

GEOFF. That's okay.

DONNY. Or hurt anyone. And I think I've scared and hurt people before.

TRAE. Yeah.

DONNY. And.
I think. If I feel too much. I might.
Explode.

GEOFF. Maybe.

TRAE. But. We're here.

GEOFF *and* TRAE *back away.*

DONNY *is alone.*
DONNY *is terrified, like a little boy looking for his parent.*

Silence. Then.

B (*from the audience*). Donny. Donny. Donny. Donny! Donny! Donny! Donny! Donny! Donny!

TRAE *and* GEOFF *join.*
The whole audience joins.

TRAE *and* GEOFF *quiet the crowd down.*
They watch.

My god. Is this what it takes to get a grown man to dance?

In this moment, we might realize that we haven't seen DONNY *smile once in this play.*

The man has done so much wrong in his life.
He is responsible for it all.
He could have been better, but he wasn't.
He could have been different, but he isn't.

But he can be. It's the 'can be.'
The possibility. It fills him up.
Oh my god it fills him up.

DONNY *moves his arms a little bit.*
Then his shoulders.

He suddenly does a squat.
I don't know what that was. DONNY *doesn't know what that was.*
He does a little kick.

He jumps up and down and turns.
He jumps like he is cheering for himself.

He lets out a weird noise. Not a shout. Not a laugh.
Like a human discovering his voice for the first time.

He keeps moving.

Now he can't stop. Now he's losing control.

It's not really dancing.
It's mostly a lot of jumping and gesturing.

TRAE. Oh my god?

GEOFF. Yo what the –

DONNY *grabs* GEOFF *and shakes him and spins him around.*
DONNY *grabs* TRAE *and hugs him and they jump together.*

DONNY *is still not smiling.*
He is moving like he doesn't know what his body is capable of.
Like he has never met his own body before.
Like he can't believe he even has a body still.

SUDDENLY HE IS IN THE AUDIENCE.

HE IS TWIRLING AND DANCING AND MOVING AND FREE.

HIS BEAST.

HE GETS AUDIENCE MEMBERS TO DANCE WITH HIM.

TRAE *AND* GEOFF *JOIN AND DO THE SAME.*

Now finally a bit of music can play.
Now finally DONNY *can smile.*

From the audience, B. *giggles.*
B. *laughs.*
B.*'s laugh starts to grow into cheers. They grow more.*

B. *is hyperventilating.*
B. *is watching these men and this audience.*
Watching them dance. Absorbing it all.
Eyes wide open.

B. *is overwhelmed by the beauty of it.*

The theater floods with laughs and giggles.

B. *feels a tingle. Like her insides are laughing.*

B. *realizes she is about to come.*

B. *is so surprised.* B. *shares the surprise with everyone around her.*
B. *can't believe it.* B. *might lean on the people next to her for support.*
B. *can't believe she is about to come with her eyes open.*

It doesn't matter what the audience is looking at.
It is all happening.

The theater floods with a mix of music and giggles and laughter and moans.

When it finishes, TRAE, GEOFF, *and* DONNY *are back onstage.*

Everything has died down.

DONNY *is exhausted. All three men are exhausted.*
More tired than they've ever been in their lives.

They look out. They see B. *who is just as tired as they are.*
The theater is in a state of disarray.

A moment.

B (*to the Dancing Bears*). Thank you for trusting me with your pleasure!

A moment.

THE DANCING BEARS. Thank you for trusting us with your pleasure!

A moment.
A moment.

End of play.

Note on Casting

Ideally, this play is as multiracial as possible.
Some things I can say for certain:

GEOFF is Black.
B. is Black or a person of color.
TRAE is most likely a non-Black person of color.
DONNY is most likely white, but can be played by an actor of any race so long as that actor could reasonably be B.'s father.

A Nick Hern Book

Tender first published in Great Britain in 2026 as a paperback original by Nick Hern Books Limited, The Glasshouse, 49a Goldhawk Road, London W12 8QP, in association with Soho Theatre, London

Cover image: Unsplash

Designed and typeset by Nick Hern Books, London
Printed in Great Britain by Mimeo Ltd, Huntingdon, Cambridgeshire PE29 6XX

A CIP catalogue record for this book is available from the British Library

ISBN 978 1 83904 536 3

Woodland CARBON
www.woodlandcarbon.co.uk
NICK HERN BOOKS
Printed on Carbon Captured paper

www.nickhernbooks.co.uk/environmental-policy

Nick Hern Books' authorised representative in the EU is
Easy Access System Europe – Mustamäe tee 50, 10621 Tallinn, Estonia
email gpsr.requests@easproject.com